/- /9 -93

PENGUIN BOOKS

IAN SHOALES' PERFECT WORLD

After receiving MFA degrees in playwriting and fiction from the University of Iowa, Merle Kessler moved to San Francisco with Duck's Breath Mystery Theatre in 1976. His collaborations with the Ducks run the media gamut from stage and radio to television. His plays have been produced at the Williamstown Theatre Festival in Massachusetts, the One Act Theatre Company of San Francisco, the Bay Area Playwrights Festival, the Denver Center for the Performing Arts, the Hawkeye Space in Berkeley, and the Dance Theatre Workshop in New York City, among others. A collection of Ian Shoales' commentaries, *I Gotta Go*, was published in 1985 by Putnam/Perigee; he is the coauthor (with Dan Coffey) of *The Official Dr. Science Big Book of Science* (Contemporary, 1987). Kessler is presently working on a novel, a screenplay, and a musical, *Suicide Blonde*. He is married, with a stepdaughter, a daughter, and a dog.

Ian Shoales' commentaries have aired on NPR's "All Things Considered," "Nightline," "Showtime," NCTV, and VH-1, among other audio/visual venues, and have appeared in print in *USA Today*, the Minneapolis *Star Tribune*, the *Washington Post*, and *Mademoiselle*. A confirmed bachelor, Mr. Shoales spends his spare time tearing down without building up, and searching for ways to improve his miserable lifestyle. He hopes that a starring role in a movie is not far behind.

IAN SHOALES'

Perfect World

by MERLE KESSLER

Penguin Books

PENGUIN BOOKS
Published by the Penguin Group
Viking Penguin Inc., 40 West 23rd Street,
New York, New York 10010, U.S.A.
Penguin Books Ltd, 27 Wrights Lane,
London W8 5TZ, England
Penguin Books Australia Ltd, Ringwood,
Victoria, Australia
Penguin Books Canada Ltd., 2801 John Street,
Markham, Ontario, Canada L3R 1B4
Penguin Books (N.Z.) Ltd, 182–190 Wairau Road,
Auckland 10, New Zealand

Penguin Books Ltd, Registered Offices:
Harmondsworth, Middlesex, England

First published in Penguin Books 1988
Published simultaneously in Canada

10 9 8 7 6 5 4 3 2 1

LIBRARY OF CONGRESS CATALOGING IN PUBLICATION DATA
Shoales, Ian, 1949–
Ian Shoales' perfect world.
1. United States—Social life and customs—
1971–   —Anecdotes, facetiae, satire, etc.   I. Title.
II. Title: Perfect world.
E169.02.S4844   1988   973.92   87-29216
ISBN 0 14 01.0003 2

Printed in the United States of America by
R. R. Donnelley & Sons Company, Harrisonburg, Virginia
Set in Meridien
Designed by Beth Tondreau Design/Carol Barr

for Mary, goddess

Food for Thought

Far be it from me to disparage our craft, whereby we have our living! Only we must note these things: that Reviewing spreads with strange vigour; that such a man as Byron reckons the Reviewer and the Poet equal; that at the last Leipzig Fair, there was advertised a Review of Reviews. By and by it will be found that all Literature has become one boundless self-devouring Review . . .

—Thomas Carlyle, 1831

Parts of this book first appeared, in slightly different form, in San Francisco Focus *magazine. Also a smattering of commentaries, aired on National Public Radio's "All Things Considered," have been transcribed and shamelessly incorporated into this book. Thanks must be paid to Steve Baker, Brad Bunnin, and Kathryn Court for their work on behalf of this book; to Jim Turner for letting me borrow Randee; and to the city of Los Angeles for graciously allowing itself to be the butt of my jokes.*

foreword

Sure, you're right, it's easy to find flaws. "Sure," America says to the critic, "it's easy for you to break a few eggs, but where's your omelet? You can tear down, but you can't build up, can you? The suffering and labor of the artist mean nothing to you, do they Mr. Ian Shoales? You don't believe in anything," America screams, "except the sound of your own voice!" Well, calm down, America. Lighten up. Unclench those hardworking fists.

I admit it freely—I'm not a positive thinker. On "Star Trek" the beautiful alien with green hair and taut belly would always say to Captain Kirk, "Oh one called Jim, what is this thing you call a kiss?" If that alien were here today (and in my Perfect World, believe me, she would be), she would gaze at me lovingly and say, "Oh one called Ian, what is this thing you call a sneer?" That's the kind of guy I am. Captain Kirk and I both want the same thing: the whole-hearted devotion of a naive alien. And if certain things stand in our way—Klingons for Kirk, reality for me—well, we just have to suck in our guts, set the phasers on Stun, and hope for the best.

The crucial difference, then, between a starship commander and social critic is *attitude.* My attitude is bad. That's why, here in Starship America, I'm not in command of anything but my own faculties. I'm just another crew member—not, however, the anonymous crew member who beams down to the planet's surface to get zapped by the Unseen Menace, no. Dr. McCoy will never stand over *this* guy's body to say, "He's dead, Jim," and set the creaky plot in motion. Nope, I'm the crew member who calls the boss a jerk whenever his back is turned. I'm the crew member who almost washed out at the Academy. I'm the crew member who's got a little something going on the side: black-market Dilithium crystals, maybe, or anonymous pamphlets urging the crew to mutiny. I'm the John Cassavetes figure. I snuck into the set from another movie. I'm just not motivated. I don't *want* to beam down to the planet's surface, okay? I want to be left alone on the bridge with Uhura. To abandon this Star Trek metaphor (if not the green-haired alien), I'm the guy who hates everything you like.

When I was a kid growing up in the Midwest, I used to entertain a fantasy: I'd be walking out on the prairie with my binoculars, trying to find the tree, when suddenly I would trip over a magic lamp. I'd rub the lamp, and a genie would appear to grant me my three wishes, which were: (1) *Get me the hell out of the Midwest.* (2) *Tell me how the world works.* (3) *Give me lots of money.*

I was just a kid. I didn't think the latter two goals were mutually exclusive. I thought I could show up at a job interview and say, "I wanna figure out how the world works. Can you start me out at sixty thou a year, with perks?" It just doesn't work that way. There is no interface between curiosity and greed. And if I *had* released a genie, it probably would have flown me directly to Iran, where I would be held hostage until the U.S. government coughed up a stealth bomber. And if you think the U.S. government would swap a sophisticated weapon for this malignant citizen, you've got another think coming. Sabu (*The Thief of Bagdad,* 1940) didn't have these problems.

But Sabu got out of show business, and I grew up. I did indeed get the hell out of the Midwest, and I learned a few things. I learned, for example, that a man with tattoos is seldom a tourist. I learned that the incidence of cups of coffee consumed in soap operas is directly proportional to the incidence of high-speed car chases on prime-time television. And cruelest of all, I've learned that the bucks in this criticism thing just aren't what they should be. I figure if I'm not gonna make any jack in my chosen profession, the least I can do is vent my spleen. My motto is *Vent for those who can't.*

Back in 1964, I was among the millions who attended the World's Fair in New York. One of the exhibits there (besides the Television on the Head of a Pin, the Subterranean Ranch-Style Home, and the Kitchen of Tomorrow) was Michelangelo's *Pieta.* To see this sculpture I waited forty-five minutes in line, then stood on a conveyor belt packed with art gawkers, which whisked us past the *Pieta* in just under a minute, while Gregorian chants were loudly piped in over hidden loudspeakers. If I'd blinked twice, I would have missed the frozen grief of Christ's mother. If this is how we admire the so-called *best* that Western culture has to offer, why should we even worry about what's the worst? I dunno. Just venting.

But maybe aesthetic appreciation, like drug addiction, is just a parody of success (*the* art form of the eighties). Consider: the successful person wheels and deals in order to achieve a success that is not complete in itself, but is only the stepping-stone to ever larger successes. Just so with the art gawker, who experiences the art and has the epiphany, then looks around for more. And so with the addict, who spends the day frantically scrounging enough money through robbery and con games to buy a tiny piece of heaven in a needle or a snort, a little orgasm gone as soon as you get it. There's never enough. Never. Not in Western culture. There's no end to this materialist road, just a theoretical logical extreme: in the Perfect World, the Perfect Work of Art (like the uncut stuff, like the master stroke in the boardroom) should kill you.

I don't want that responsibility. So forget art, success, drugs; let's talk about *me*. This "one called me" will be the subject of this book. And what *is* this book? Well, it won't have footnotes, I'll tell you that.[1] Perhaps we could call this book a "fictionalization," which would be to a real novel what a "novelization" is to a movie, or what "colorization" is to color. Call it what you like. All I know is, I got my advance from the publishers so I call it a "legal obligation." The primary purpose of American society is to keep lawyers busy, so I'll do my part. I may be cranky, but, like Captain Kirk, I take my obligations seriously.

So don't worry, oh one called consumer, you'll get your money's worth. The purifying rain of hard-hitting social criticism, the smooth ice of polished prose, the stream of consciousness—it's all here, folks. I have assembled the Utopian Legos. If you want to put them together and move in, hey, that's up to you.

But I'll tell you this: if this puppy doesn't net me a Pulitzer, or at the very least one of those genius grants, I'm gonna get out of the opinion game and go into screenwriting. You don't need opinions to write movies—as a matter of fact, they're a detriment.

So save me from myself, America, and follow me. I am hostage to my own fate. You don't need a stealth bomber to rescue me. Just turn the page. Let us boldly go where no one has gone before. As the roadies say before the concert, "Let's carve this turkey."

[1]Except this one.

preface

The following is an edited transcript of a meeting held on January third, 1988, in the twenty-fourth floor conference room of the PetroDyne Building in downtown San Francisco, where freelance social critic Ian Shoales was occupying a minor position with that corporation through the auspices of the Con-TempoRare Agency. Minutes after this meeting was concluded, Mr. Shoales was dismissed (unfairly) from that position, ostensibly for using the conference room without permission during the Executive Vice President's lunch hour. Mr. Shoales, who at that time needed that position and consequent paycheck quite desperately, hopes that both ConTempoRare and PetroDyne die, go to hell, and burn in flames till the end of time.

This meeting was recorded illegally on a Wollensak reel-to-reel tape recorder which had been left in the basement of Mr. Shoales' apartment building, along with some albums and stuff, by a fleeing cocaine dealer; it was found by Mr. Shoales, and concealed under the very large conference table subsequent to the aforesaid consequent meeting.

It is Mr. Shoales' fervid hope that the conferees will not sue him for using these clandestine recordings without their permission; he begs to remind them that, legally speaking, one cannot get blood from a stone. If the conferees *should* choose to sue Mr. Shoales, Mr. Shoales hopes they all die, go to hell, and burn in flames till the end of time.

If they leave Mr. Shoales alone, he will wish them well. He even will wish to inform them that their checks are in the mail. Mr. Shoales begins the meeting.

SHOALES

I'd like to thank all of you for the work you've put into *Ian Shoales' Perfect World*. As you know, I wanted to write this book by myself, but you just can't do things alone anymore. You gotta protect yourself. Some of you already know each other, but I thought we'd go around the room, have each of you introduce yourselves, and explain if you would your contribution to *Ian Shoales' Perfect World*. Misha Jones, go ahead.

MISHA

Thanks, Ian. I'm a freelance marketing consultant. I worked with Sandra Nelson—stand up, Sandy—who did the packaging. Our job was to create a concept that both Ian Shoales and the mainstream American consumer could tolerate. So far, that tolerance level has been just tremendous.

SANDY

We wanted this to be unlike anything people have ever read before, but we didn't want it to be "way out," like those French things some of you may have read in college. So we set up a Creativity Committee, a kind of focus group—

SHOALES

Less work for me, haw haw!

SANDY

—to set up a humor gauge with our target audience. This was to insure that the humor would always interface with commercial potential—

MISHA

—We wanted to stay within that area where advertising can impact—

SANDY

Right, Misha! Then I put all the research together between leatherette covers, with salmon-colored stitching and raised violet letters, and we sent this off to potential sponsors and underwriters, then followed through with phone calls.

MISHA

Of course a lot of that follow-through fell through.

SANDY

You have to expect that. Originally *Ian Shoales' Perfect World* was going to be a multimedia event: book package, video package, CD, movie, play-set—

MISHA

I thought the Ian Shoales action figure was just darling, myself.

SANDY

Unfortunately it made small children shudder.

MISHA

We still have hopes.

SANDRA

We just have to adopt a Wait-And-See! Thank you!

SHOALES

The tweedy gent next to Sandy is Ernie Doyle. Speak right into the flowers there and describe your input into this output.

ERNEST

My name is Ernest Cromwell Doyle. I have a PhD in comparative literature. My function here is to deconstruct the text as we go along.

SHOALES

He's here to second-guess the critics.

ERNEST

In a sense. Although evaluation, as such, is a sentimental anachronism—

SHOALES

He's here to help the reader understand what's going on.

ERNEST

Well, no. Every text is merely an operation, a kind of event—

SHOALES

Dream on, white boy. Next we have Code Name Omega. We can't reveal his true identity. He's worked with the NSC, the CIA, and the FBI, both covertly and overtly. His specialty is disinformation, which I thought would come in mighty handy in a work of fiction. When the latest White House operation was revealed, he was fed to the wolves. He's on the run from his own employers, and he needed the work. Is that essentially correct, Omega?

OMEGA

I am not at liberty to reveal that information at the present time.

SHOALES

Take off that nose putty, Omega, you're only fooling yourself. Next to Omega is Professor Nancy Cordell, historian.

NANCY

These are hard times for history professors.

SHOALES

Well, it's good to have you on the team. Next is my attorney, Nick Further, who keeps me updated on the latest libel laws. This is *very* important when creating a Perfect World.

NICK

Let's keep this moving. I have a meeting with a real client at one.

SHOALES

All right now, this is the team that provided the structure and authenticity necessary for any Utopian fantasy. But what about that animating spark? I needed visionaries. And I got them. Floyd?

FLOYD

My name is Floyd Washington. I am a custodian in South San Francisco. For the past twenty years, in my spare time, I have been creating a meeting place for the Last Judgment in my garage, using only aluminum foil and lawn furniture. Flee from the wrath to come.

SHOALES

I sure will, Floyd, and it's great to have you with us. Next we have our own channel to the spirits of the past, my favorite medium, Sister Kitty.

KITTY

Whom do you wish to summon, seeker?

SHOALES

No one today, babe, thanks. For help with certain technical aspects of necromancy and time travel, we have theoretical physicist, Dr. Albert Britt.

ALBERT

This beats working on SDI, I guess, but not by much.

SHOALES

With Al on board, the laws of physics just won't get in the way. To keep this whole thing completely scientific, I've got my very own control group: Ralph, a guy I met on the street—

RALPH

How are ya? I think your book will be terrific, by the way, and I'm not much of a reader.

SHOALES

That about sums up the crew, with one exception, my prose stylist Kapler, or Keefler, who chose not to appear here. I figured I needed a professional writer for some of the more lyrical moments in this sucker, so I hired this Keffler or Kreisler, I can never remember his name. He only took cash and I only used him a couple times. A couple *sentences* really, and he wanted five hundred bucks. I ask you, did I get my money's worth?

MISHA

He's been *paid?*

NICK

You haven't been paid either?

FLOYD

He told me *you* had a check for me.

KITTY

Where's *my* money?

SHOALES

Don't look at me that way, Omega. Hold your horses, everybody—

SOUND OF HEAVY DOOR OPENING.

VOICE OF EXECUTIVE VICE PRESIDENT

What's going on here? Shoales, you idiot!

INAUDIBLE, GARBLED, EXPLETIVES DELETED, PORTION OF TAPE MISSING, UNINTELLIGIBLE

PART ONE

Ugly Realities

in which we clutch at final straws and break
the camel's back

Food for Thought

Oh, Time, Strength, Cash, and Patience.

—Herman Melville, *Moby Dick*

picture perfect

How did my life end up like this?

It seems like only yesterday—it *was* yesterday is why—I was sitting poolside in Hollywood with a singer from Nashville, a very thin young woman named Lucille, who volunteered the information that she'd dumped her Tennessee writing partner (and lover) on the strength of a vague compliment and a business card, which she held away from the pool, gingerly, two-fingered, and out of the sun, the way one holds something delicate or potentially dangerous.

Somewhere between Nashville and L.A. the business card had lost some of its crisp perfection. It was crimped in one corner, like the ringer in Three-Card Monte, and it said simply MURRAY & MURRAY. What Murray & Murray could do for Lucille was not clear from the card, but Lucille was too confident in her abilities to worry about that. She thought they could probably get her in the movies. Nothing big at first. Maybe singing in the background, a bar scene in a Clint Eastwood. She didn't care which star, really. Burt Reynolds even, or one of those new kids, those *Top Gun* types. Even a brat-pack wanna-be like C. Thomas Howell. Just a little bitty scene, but it would put her thin face and trembling voice square in the back brain of America. This would lead to a record contract, then (she supposed) "Star Search," then a square on the "New Hollywood Squares," a miniseries maybe, then either retirement or a sitcom, depending on how she felt. That was her plan.

What Murray & Murray had said was, "If you ever get to L.A. give us a call." That's all the encouragement Lucille needed. She ditched R.J. (her partner), sold her Buick, and shagged a Greyhound west, so she could spend half her days calling Murray & Murray (just like they asked her to), and the other half poolside with her door open, so she could hear Murray or Murray in case he should ever return her calls. (If she'd listened closely enough, she probably could have heard the drip of snowballs in hell, but I didn't tell her that.) She wrote down the time of each call to Murray & Murray in a small black book, which book was ever by her side. Her compulsive call-charting was the only detail to betray her anxiety, unless you counted her compulsive scratching. I didn't. In my opinion, the nonstop scratching was more from flea bites than nerves.

Her flea bites? The result of spending the previous night with friends of friends in the Canyon, friends of friends who eke out a living of sorts, so Lucille said, erasing the bass lines from popular tunes. This process made the tunes easy on the ears in supermarkets or elevators—even when she was put on hold while calling Murray & Murray, she thought she'd heard their work that morning as a matter of fact, isn't that exciting? Plus the friends of friends raise dogs. Hence the fleas. That was yesterday. Okay.

So last night my manager called, to ask me to go to a party up in the hills. The party-givers were a marketing consultant and his wife, who'd put away thirty mil in fiscal '85. How? Well, as near as I could follow the financial metaphysics, here's how: it seems a computer engineering firm had developed a new computer tone, which shaved nanoseconds between signal relays, increasing telecommunication volume for a certain long-distance service. This new efficiency enabled them to sell themselves to *another* long distance service, after first stripping themselves of assets so they could declare bankruptcy (*losing* billions on paper, *making* millions through a write-off). Then they all (engineers, executives, and lawyers from both firms) formed a limited partnership, bought themselves back from themselves, and made a two-billion-dollar profit, with assets amortized over ten years, just under the tax-reform wire. The host of the party had brokered this whole deal, which means (I think) that the dealmakers borrowed his office, while he went out and drank cappuccino in some trendy café.

This guy (call him Michael) was retired, rich, and bored, but not as bored as his wife (Tatiana, not her real name), who'd experienced some kind of bland religious conversion in Malibu six months before and had badgered her husband into giving her five million dollars to promote her brainstorm: a multimedia coast-to-coast campaign that *had no product* (now there's a concept, pals and gals, kind of like poetry, only more expensive and time-consuming), it only had an attitude, or slogan, which was *Feel Good about You*. Michael and Tatiana had heard one of my incisive commentaries on the radio, and wanted me to be incisive for *them*. Or, as my manager said Tatiana had said, they would love to have me "aboard" to keep the project "grounded." They wanted, in other words, a court jester to offset what they called an "audio/visualization of a Perfect World." Their goal was to create a videocassette/compact-disc package that would cause a spiritual renaissance! In the privacy of the home!

There was a potential and easy ten thousand in it for me, my manager said, if I could keep my opinions to myself for a couple hours, nod, and exchange flatteries with these airheads. I said *Sure*, being broke as usual (but we'll get to that).

When the oak doors to their modest mansion swung open, the first thing I saw was the centerpiece of their lovely home, a television screen the size of my parents' dining-room table, a table so large you had to squeeze around it to sit down. My maiden aunt Constance fainted the first time she saw this table, and woke up weeping with awe. Every Thanksgiving we would sit at this table after dinner, helpless, trapped between table and wall until our stomachs had retreated enough to squeeze back out again. For years my parents held enormous receptions, so visitors could view this table. My folks would serve coffee and cake, and guests would stand in the dining-room doorway and gawk. But twenty-some years later, in the hills of Hollywood, nobody gawked at this television. In Los Angeles, you only gawk at traffic accidents. I couldn't even gawk at my host and hostess, though God knows I wanted to. They were extremely gawkable—the Perfect Couple. They dazzled with blondness, Michael and Tatiana did, from hair to shoes.

"Please remove your tie," said Tatiana with a smile, as her sullen maid escorted me into her presence, "and join the others in the viewing pit."

The others were the usual Hollywood motley: a couple of middle-aged guys wondering whether they should light their cigars or not; a young Turk or two with a tapered briefcase; a blonde bimbo, squinting because her tinted contacts were out of whack; two production assistants named Wolf and Hypatia, with toothy grins, and legs that twitched like the tendons of a galvanized frog in a ninth-grade biology class. The tension in the air was disguised as relaxation. "Disguised tension" pretty much describes any social event in Los Angeles. Everybody sat, Not Smoking, on enormous Chinese pillows.

"They're from Formosa, actually," said Michael, indicating the pillows with a languid wave of a manicured hand. "I had them designed especially for this space by Li Tuan. The last of the old craftspersons. Very ancient. Very wise. Chips?"

He nodded his head at a series of tiny porcelain bowls, each containing no more than six bright yellow chips of something.

"They're sun-dried cactus slices," he said. "From a little Navajo bakery I know. Very edible. Please. Enjoy. Sit. Whatever. *Mi casa es su casa.*"

I knelt on a pillow displaying dragons devouring dragons, next to a music researcher from Van Nuys, as I learned, who looked as out of place as I felt.

"The name's Bob," he murmured. "But you'd better call me Robert. Looks like that kind of night."

The soft indirect lighting dimmed to nothing. Wind-chimes tinkled and the presentation began. On the vast television screen, our hostess appeared, making a semi-sinuous attempt at a Dance Poem, accompanied by inappropriately deafening jazz, the kind of pointless noodling you hear late Sunday nights on public radio. Every once in a while, a seagull was superimposed over Tatiana's face, and fast-motion films of cars on freeways. It was real *Koyaanisqatsi* stuff.

After an eternity the lights came back up. We all made comments, favorable. "Interesting," was as much as I could muster. Tiny increments of white wine were served.

Then the hostile maid appeared before the gathering with little beakers on a silver platter. This must have been a cue, because a lean, balding man leaped up from his pillow and put his hands on his hips like a drill instructor.

"Okay people, listen up," he said, his voice cracking. "We want you to enjoy yourselves. I'm Dennis, your attorney on this thing, and *I* want you to enjoy yourselves. But—"

He flashed a fleeting bright grin that betrayed years of practice.

"—you must be free to work on this project. Not only spiritually free—" He nodded at Tatiana, who bowed her head in return. "—but drug-free as well. Please, people, urinalysis is not an accusation, it's merely a precaution. Insurance demands it, Legal demands it, Michael and Tatiana request it.''

The maid thrust her platter at me with a scowl.

"Wait a minute," I said.

"Joost tayk de bottle mon," said the maid from the corner of her mouth.

"This is exciting!" said the squinting bimbo, taking a bottle.

Michael touched my shoulder gently.

"You have quibbles," he said. "I respect that. We want a quibbles person on the team, but I'm afraid this is necessary."

"Necessary isn't the right word," I said. "I think the word you want is 'stupid.' ''

"Let me get this straight," said Dennis. He chopped at the air with his hands. "Just so we're all clear on this point. You are *not* going to participate in this test?"

Oh cripes, I thought, *I've done it again.*

"Are you on drugs *now*?" he asked gravely.

Kiss it good-bye. "I'm sorry this didn't work out," I said.

Dennis turned to Michael and Tatiana. "*If* he's on drugs—and I'm not saying he is—but *if* he is, and he has an accident driving down the hill, you are potentially liable. Frankly, your Perfect World Project doesn't need that kind of publicity."

Michael gave me a gentle frown.

"Can I have my tie back?" I asked the maid.

She turned to get it.

"Hold it, Sarah," said Michael. The maid froze in her tracks. He turned to me. "We can't let you leave in the condition you may or may not be in, until the drugs you may or may not have taken have or have not worn off. I mean *have* worn off. Allegedly."

"You can't keep me here," I protested.

"Get the Uzi, darling," said Michael.

"Yeah," I sneered. "*Get the Uzi, darling*. I don't think you'll shoot me. I don't think you have the guts!"

I'd heard that line in a movie once. In the movie, the guy who'd said the line had been shot dead. I hoped the present situation was more New Age than Roaring Twenties.

Dennis the attorney said nervously, "You can't shoot him. He's a guest. You can only shoot intruders."

Tatiana gave me a vague hopeful look, wishing, perhaps, that I'd do something intrusive.

"Look," said Dennis. "Why don't *I* give the guy a ride?"

"What about *my* car?" I asked. "Who drives that?"

"Damn," said Dennis.

"I'll drive you," said Robert, my musician friend, heroically stepping forward.

"And Sarah will drive Robert's car," said Michael.

"What a threel dot weel be," said Sarah, deadpan.

"Great!" said Dennis. "I get to drive my own car."

"You don't have to go now," said Tatiana.

"Oh," said Dennis. "Wait. I'd better tag along as a witness."

"How far do we need to take him?" said Tatiana, examining me.

"Casinos," said Michael. "Isn't there some law with offshore casinos?"

"Three-mile limit!" said Dennis. Everyone looked relieved.

So. We synchronized our odometers and headed down the hill. Bob (or Robert) was leading in my rented car, Sarah following in Robert's car, and Dennis bringing up the rear in his BMW, his flashers flashing for reasons known only to him.

Robert said he might have an angle for me on a writing job for cable television, if I didn't mind making jokes about breasts. I said I probably minded. He said he was gathering theme music for some cable show; he was looking for tunes in the public domain that would still sound good on a Yamaha DX-7.

"They used different changes back then, man," he said. "Stephen Foster and Philip Glass might as well be from different planets. Here's three miles. I'm gonna pull over."

We exchanged vehicles and phone numbers. Dennis the attorney sat behind his wheel, shaking his head slowly back and forth in rhythm (so it seemed to me) with his flashers. He never took his eyes off me. Sarah, the Jamaican maid, never looked at me at all. I drove off, leaving them all behind me.

future perfect

In my *Film Encyclopedia* (Ephraim Katz, Perigee, New York, 1979)—well, okay, it's not mine, I borrowed it from a friend—a *flashforward* is defined as

> . . . a scene in a motion picture representing an event that is . . . imagined to occur later than the one currently depicted. This narrative device . . . can be quite useful in the futuristic structure of science fiction stories or in depicting the hopes and dreams of a character.

Well, that's what we have here, gentle reader, a glimpse of the hopes and dreams of a character. I can see why the flashforward isn't used much in the movies (movies are pretty linear, really, when you think about it), but for the labyrinthine depths of the printed word, wow! The flashforward just can't be beat. It's unique, it adds a little spice to the prose style, and it's a breezy little display of technique for its own sake. *I like it, J.B., and I think the kids will like it too*.

So let's install this camera on the hood of my rented Fury (Dial-A-Heap Rentals, eighteen bucks a day), and pan over to the driver, me. Bang in tight. There. We see an extreme close-up of my face, intense and drawn, etched in deep shadow as I leave Michael and Tatiana behind, and steer down into the City of Angels, down through intermittent pools of yellow streetlight. Very moving. Very *noir*.

Suddenly ripples pass over the windshield, like the traces of a pebble dropped into a still pond. Harp arpeggios on the soundtrack. My face vanishes, the screen goes black. We fade in on—what? My face? Again? I'm a little older, but not much. There are distinguished streaks of gray at my temples, and the trace, the ghost of a smile. But why is this face so still? We pull back. Whoa. *Nice* suit. I've come up in the world. Hmmmm. I seem to be—why *yes*, I'm made of wax! It must be the figure of me in some wax museum. What in the—? But wait. We move the camera back slightly, and see that this is a *photograph* of my likeness in wax. It's a postcard. A postcard? Let's flip it over. What does it say?

Up there in the left-hand corner: *"Is it live or is it Memorex?"* It says, "He's so real you could swear he's about to sneer, and he's just one of thousands of figures at *Ian Shoales' Perfect World of Wax*, located on Bobcat Shudder Road, one mile off the coastal highway, between San Luis Obispo and Watsonville."

Ah yes. Some folks dream of picket fences, and hippies by the fire. Some dream of being a friend, on the side of the road, to man. Some dream of condos and big fish, golf and world peace, social work and bridge. Me? I just want a little wax museum on a little hill by the sea, a wax museum with an attitude, a wax museum that dares to tell the truth, a wax museum that will rip the lid off corruption and foolishness, a wax museum that will realize at last the potential wax musea have always had: to become *high art!* And why not? The wax likeness of a famous figure does the same thing as a photograph, only in three dimensions. Photography is considered art. Well, wax gives you *more* for your buck, *plus* wax figures take longer to make. Even *high* art's gotta factor in the labor.

Ian Shoales' Perfect World of Wax. A foolish dream? Perhaps, but when I close my eyes, I can just see the gift shop, the ample parking . . .

But there's more here than meets the eye. Move your eye down the postcard. There's a message, it's my handwriting: *My dearest Ruth, my world is Almost Perfect now. All it lacks is you. XXX Ian.* Yeah, that's right. Even Ian Shoales can sap out over a dame. Even a wax museum can melt, resolve itself into a dew—enough of this. Forgive me. This ain't no *ordinary* dame, folks. This is the Perfect Woman. Whoops, we're almost home. We'll get back to the future later.

our narrative resumes

———————————————— Okay. Now. Where I was staying in L.A. was at this complex of apartments, which was one of many rental properties owned by a self-made millionaire whom we will call Fiskel Yahr. I was staying in his apartment while he was in New York negotiating for a skyscraper or something. He had flats in San Francisco and New York, in Atlanta, two in Dallas, a winter place in Florida, two summer places in Aspen and Bozeman, and a place on an island in a sea whose name he couldn't even remember.

Fiskel, a slight furry man with tiny hands, had his fingers in many pies. How we became acquainted was, he'd heard me on the radio and wanted to hire me to write and perform a series of radio commercials that would say nasty things about a certain product he wished to sell. Badmouthing his own product, he thought, would be catchy advertising, and would make America think he was a good guy who could take a joke. That was his strategy, anyway. But before we go any further, let's take a look at the commentary he heard, shall we?

op/ed from ian

"Garbage Pail Kids"

The other day I was listening to some radio talk show, and a guy called in, all bent out of shape, because they were making shoes for kids with Velcro straps instead of laces. He was afraid if these things caught on, kids wouldn't know how to tie their shoes anymore. Well jeeze, I thought, if we don't have shoes with laces anymore, what's the *value* in knowing how to tie your shoes? It's like getting upset because they don't have blacksmiths in a Nike factory.

But this nation hungry for bland controversies has a new one: Garbage Pail Kids. This is your basic bubble-gum card, each of which show a kid as a monster, mutated beyond description. Parents are upset about Garbage Pail Kids, naturally. Some grocers refuse to carry them. Kids, of course, love them.

And anytime a kid starts to have fun in America, there are bandwagons full of the alarmed ready to jump on the fun, then churn out a thin, terribly written best-seller about the negative psychological side effects of fun: that fun is sexist, that fun is racist, that fun will stunt a kid's growth, that fun has no practical value, that fun promotes a poor self-image— I say let the kids have the damn bubble-gum cards. Don't we have anything important to worry about?

We Baby Boomers are busy bringing babies into the world, and acting like we're the first people in history to have this bright idea. We bring the same self-absorption to the simple act of propagation as we do to the selection of a sushi bar. We got Harvard prep preschools, we got prenatal language tapes, we got infant fashions . . .

Let me explain something to you about Garbage Pail Kids. They're popular because they're a parody of Cabbage Patch Kids, which are a parody of real kids. As a matter of fact, I heard Cabbage Patch is suing Garbage Pail. Is this like a Smurf suing a Gremlin? I don't know. But I know this: a kid with a Cabbage Patch Kid is rehearsing to be a grown-up. A kid with a Garbage Pail Kid is just being a kid, doing his or her little job: annoying parents. Yes, this is yet another so-called "moral dilemma" that isn't moral at all. It's merely a difference in taste, that's all, a kind of art snobbery. Parents only hate Garbage Pail Kids because they're not Cabbage Patch Kids. In other words, they're the wrong kind of ugly. I gotta go.

---

the story continued
The millionaire, upon hearing the preceding commentary, summoned me to his San Francisco offices on Union

14

Street. His British secretary gave me a cup of coffee, and I was set down in a conference room. Fiskel sat across from me. He plunked an object in front of me, then leaned back with hands folded and head tilted. He watched me bemusedly as I examined the object.

It was a fuzzy gray thing about a foot and a half high. It had a built-in microcassette recorder with a voice-activated microphone. When you talked to it, your own voice would come back at you thirty seconds later, filtered and speeded-up, so you sounded like a psychotic chipmunk. The instructions, written in tortured English, said that it came with adapters and could function as an answering machine.

"What the hell is this supposed to be?" I asked. "A bear? A monkey? A weasel?"

"Some cute thing," he said. "I've got five hundred thousand of them in a warehouse I just bought in New Jersey. They were part of the property. If I could unload them for a profit, I'd be a very happy guy. I've got some Korean telephoto lenses coming in, and I need the room."

"Maybe it's supposed to be a Russian," I said.

"I don't know what the hell it is," said Fiskel. "I just want to get rid of them. I'll leave you alone with it for a half hour, and we'll see what we come up with."

He left me alone to contemplate this thing. As I worked, I recalled Fiskel's name from some article I'd read. He'd tried to buy CBS using NBC stock, even though he owned no NBC stock. "But I *would* have," he had explained to the SEC, "if they'd accepted my offer."

After a half hour, Fiskel returned, and I turned on the bear.

"Hi!" it said. "I'm an idea from hell, spawned by a synapse glitch, a hitch in the collective unconscious, assembled by underpaid Asian workers, and shipped to America, where people will buy anything, as long as it doesn't cross that thin line between cute and demonic. Batteries not included! Have a *nice* day!" I switched it off.

Fiskel drummed his fingers and nodded thoughtfully. "I like it. I like the contempt. I like the scope of the contempt. I think we're on to something here."

He stood up and paced. The beeper on his belt went off. Four lines on the telephone lit up. He switched off the beeper. He said into the phone, "Hold all calls." He hung up and looked at me. I *liked* that.

"Here's the deal," he said. "I gotta fly east and then go to L.A. I'll fly you to L.A. and put you up at my place in Hollywood. I'm gonna turn you loose on this thing but," he held up a hand, "I don't want any money changing hands yet."

"God forbid I get paid for this," I said.

"It's not like that," he said. "This whole promotion campaign could come very close to libel. It's a legal gray area, and I don't want to be forced to sue you. We need to set up some joint ownership deal, a production company, like that. That way, if the legal department objects, my only recourse would be to sue myself."

"Can you sue yourself?" I asked.

"Oh sure," he said, "but I only do it when I'm desperate for a write-off. Let me get back to you."

While he and his lawyers were busy working things out, I was busy getting kicked out of my girlfriend's apartment, and her life (but we'll get to that). Fiskel flew me to L.A. where I stayed in his apartment for free, and tried out sample copy on him over the telephone.

"Cross a dust bunny with an answering machine, and what do you get?" I asked. "You get Fuzzball Creephead, the toy for adults, more evidence that the world is even dumber than we dreamed, and that a guy or gal with disposable income will dispose it on anything."

"That's good," he said from his New York penthouse. "That's mean. But I think we can get meaner."

So there we were, and there I was, returning home from Michael and Tatiana's Perfect World party. It was three A.M. by the time I reached the gate of the complex and the place was crawling with cops. It seems there was a crisis going on. It seems Lucille, my poolside folksinger (remember her? Murray & Murray? You gotta keep up with me, folks, we got a lot of ground to cover in this thing), it seems Lucille had made a suicide attempt by shredding and devouring her own demo tapes. The paramedics were pumping her stomach, and the police, in responding to the 911, had not only found an illegal alien delivering a pizza, but a couple *with a child*. This was an adults-only complex (no smokers, no pets). The police had heard the child cry out when they'd broken down Lucille's door, and the SWAT team was busy putting the family's possessions out on the street.

A bubble-helmeted cop held a machine gun, blocking my way and demanding ID. I didn't know what to do. The night manager was off monitoring these crises, and he didn't like me anyway. My driver's license was not only expired, it showed my San Francisco address. If I was going to sleep in the rich man's bed that night, I'd have to do some fast talking.

Fortunately, I didn't have to. A thin young man with long dank hair stepped up to the officer and said, "You got to let me in there. I come all the way from Tennessee to see my baby, and my baby's been hurt."

"R.J.?" I asked.

He looked at me suspiciously. "I don't know you, man," he said.

"Lucille talked about you," I said.

"You're that Murray," he said, squinting, "ain't you?"

"No," I said, "I'm just—"

"What have you done with my baby?" he screamed, leaping at me. I fell to the ground, R.J. clutching my throat. He let go. I gasped for breath, I saw his pale fists come down like falling moons.

Then three cops came out of nowhere and wrestled him away. While they were thus distracted, I went through the open gate. *What a slick move,* I thought, rubbing my throat and gagging as I stumbled through the door. *I'll have to remember this trick the next time my place is surrounded by cops. All I need is a homicidal hillbilly hippie and hey, I'm in like Flynn.*

I locked the door behind me. The phone's message light was flashing. I ignored it for a few minutes, trying to find something to eat. There was nothing in the fridge but cottage cheese on the far side of bad, a shriveled pear, and a black banana. I had seven bucks in my pocket, which I probably needed for gas. It was too late to get food anyway, and even if I could order a pizza, the SWAT team would probably shoot the delivery boy on sight.

I turned on the answering machine.

The first message was from the self-made Fiskel Yahr himself: "Ian, here where you call me 'human scum,' can we change that

17

to 'slime'? Don't respond now. Sleep on it. If you have no problem with that, call me in Atlanta tomorrow after three. Ciao." Click. Buzz.

Next, my manager: "This is the last straw, Ian." His voice was chilly. "I don't appreciate being awakened at two o'clock in the morning by potential clients asking about your drug problem. Find yourself another manager." Click. Buzz.

"Ian? This is Phil. I just got the bill for the credit card you borrowed. You're two hundred dollars over the limit. The rental car people are on my neck. You'd better pay that bill, and soon. I'm stopping the card. You've abused our friendship long enough." Click. Buzz.

"Ian? This is Nancy. I can't sublet your place anymore. I just can't take all the harassing phone calls. Do you owe money to everybody in San Francisco? I'm moving out. Sorry. By the way, you still owe me twenty bucks." Click. Buzz.

"This is the Midnight Collection Agency, Mr. Shoales. Last month you purchased a synthesizer, electric guitar and amp, a digital sampler, compact-disc player, and the complete *Atlantic Rhythm & Blues 1947–1974*. If we don't receive payment on these items by next week, they will be repossessed. Thank you." Click. Buzz.

"This is your landlord, Ian. Remember me? You got till tomorrow to pay the back rent, then everything's going out on the street." Click. Buzz.

"Ian, this is Kathryn at Viking. We're still waiting for the first draft of *Perfect World*. It was due six months ago, as you recall. If you can't deliver the manuscript, perhaps you'll be good enough to return our advance."

"I already spent it!" I screamed.

"Keep it down," shouted a muffled voice next door.

Click. Buzz.

"Ian? Bill. Thought I'd warn you, you're about to be sued by Hugh Hefner, Jerry Falwell, and Mr. Rogers. I told you not to run that piece. You have no case. As of now, you have no lawyer. You'll get my bill. And leave my secretary alone or I'll call the police." Click. Buzz.

"Ian Shoales, you are incapable of love." Click. Buzz.

"Ian, this is your mother. You've forgotten your father's birthday again for the tenth year in a row. He's been on the phone all day telling everybody he knows that he no longer has a son. Perhaps you should give him a call. I'll try to keep him from hanging up on you." Click. Buzz.

I felt like carrion being worried by vultures.

"Ian, this is Bob. You know, Robert? Hope you're still up. Listen, I got a gig scoring the new Chuck Norris. But I got a temp job in the morning, and it's too late to call them. You want it? You gotta be at ProCorGenTel, downtown L.A., at nine o'clock. It's just filing, but maybe you can use the bucks. Call me when you get up." Click. Buzz.

Money. The answer to my prayers. Never mind that I'd been fired from every job I'd ever had. I'd give it another shot. Mrs. Shoales didn't raise her little boy to be a quitter. Or a rememberer of fathers' birthdays.

It was twenty after five when I reset the answering machine. I could still get an hour and a half of sleep if I lay down immediately. This would still leave me alert enough to file for a day, if I napped through lunch and didn't have to answer any phones. I double-bolted the doors. Then I took every alarm clock I could find, and plugged them into the sockets next to the queen-sized downy futon. I hooked the AM/FM clock-radio into the top-of-the-line stereo system and jacked the volume up to ten. *If I don't blow out the speakers*, I thought, *that ought to wake me up.* I closed the windows and drew the shades. I pulled the curtains shut.

"What a day," I sighed as I spray-painted WAKE UP in letters a foot high on the wall opposite the bed. A Perfect Day. A Perfect End to a Perfect Day. Finally, I set the television remote-control on the coffee table, and set a coffee-table book (*The Timetables of History*, Bernard Grun, Touchstone Books, New York, 1979) on the Scan button. This would switch channels every five seconds, and give me something to watch as I drifted off. There. Whew.

So we'll get back to the book in a bit, folks, I'm just going to lie down for a few minutes. I need to recharge for an hour, that's all, just a quick little nap. Turn on the tube, watch some rapid cable, spin the dial while I drift, while I let this battered but indomitable ego disintegrate, while I rev up the REMs. This is all I need. Just a tiny little dream, and then I'm on my way.

2 HEALTHY YOU,
WEALTHY ME!—

America's favorite sunrise advice
exercise program. Hosts: Dinah
Funny, Robb Pirott.

God I'm bushed.

4 DANGEROUS YOGA—

Swami Chainsaw.

Pillow. Money. Ow.

5 WAKE UP!—

Living-room prayer breakfast.

Mmph.

perfect pitch

Commercial; 60 seconds
(BUNNIBANK)

IAN SHOALES (PRE-TAPED VOICEOVER)

This is Ian Shoales, reminding you that you're reading *Perfect World*
by Ian Shoales. We'll return to our exciting adventure after these
messages.

VIDEO	AUDIO
A BUNCH OF RABBITS SNUFFLE AROUND IN A BIG PILE OF MONEY.	ANNOUNCER (VOICEOVER) You know, money and rabbits have a lot in common. Put them together in a dark place, and they multiply.

CUT TO:

MORE RABBITS IN A BIGGER
PILE OF MONEY.

That's what banks are all
about. And that's what
BunniBank is all about.

CUT TO:

FUNNIBUNNY AUTOMATIC
TELLER SPITTING CASH FROM
ITS BUNNY MOUTH.

Making money. And having
fun.

CUT TO:

GRANDPA WALKS INTO BUNNI-
BANK. HE'S HOLDING A PUPPY
AND CHUCKLING.

BunniBank's a real friendly
place.

CUT TO:

FRECKLE-FACED BOY DUMPING
PENNIES FROM HIS PIGGY
BANK INTO THE OPEN MOUTH
OF FUNNIBUNNY AUTOMATIC
TELLER.

When you trust us with your
money, we'll do things with
it you never dreamed. And
we have the slowest attrition
rate around.

CUT TO:

BLUE-COLLAR WORKER
DANCES AND EATS A HAM-
BURGER. PEOPLE FROM ALL
WALKS OF LIFE JOIN HIM,
DANCING AND EATING HAM-
BURGERS.

And when we say that our
savings plan offers you
twenty percent annual yield,
it may not be true now, but
it *could* be. Sometime. Somehow. If we work together.
And put the glory back
where it belongs. In America.

STIRRING MUSIC.

CUT TO:

FAMILY OF FOUR STANDS
PROUDLY AGAINST A BACK-
DROP OF THE AMERICAN FLAG,
STARING FIERCELY INTO AN UN-
KNOWN YET HOPEFUL FUTURE.

So don't you owe it to yourself, and your family, to bank
Bunni?

CUT TO:

RABBIT EATING CASH.

Because money is just like a rabbit. At BunniBank, a little goes a long way.

OUT.

ANNOUNCER (VOICEOVER)

And now, back to *Perfect World*, with Ian Shoales.

(SHOW) MOVIE—

Adventure; 2 hrs. "Dragonthief-masternightwarriorbeast" (1980) Special effects highlight this tale of a beefy man's magic sword, and a woman with a bare midriff and wizard grandpa, who can turn into a dog. Rack Dirt, Suzie Woozie, Laurence Olivier.

Whuh? Zzhr. Snork.

(WTBS) (6:05) FLYING IN YOUR SLEEP—

Exercise.

Zzzzzzzz.

(21) PLANT DOCTOR—

Discussion. Cranky old geezer kills aphids.

future perfect
I can't believe it!

Here I am, high above this vast city, high above this Perfect Country, the blades of the chopper spinning so fast they can't be seen, so fast they are a reassuring hum, a mechanical mantra. Here we are in the Perfect Future at last, the future we've only dreamed about, a fantastic reality that has to be seen to be believed. Here I am, famous, respected, my name a household word. Every time my name is uttered in any household, royalty checks accrue in a numbered Swiss bank account!

I had been unhappy—yes, I admit it, unhappy. Thirty-eight and alone and poor is different from twenty-one and lonesome and broke. *Where's my ticket out of here?* I had wondered, tossing and turning on my bed of pain. But when you're down, folks, there's nowhere to go but up! Up up and away! Up! Up among the pesky seagulls, the endangered eagles, among the stately blimps and portly dirigibles that fill the sky!

My pilot is a Vietnam vet named Sarge. He knows what he's doing. He's the guy that flew the first chopper into Cambodia. He gave up a lucrative career in smuggling to work for me. Why? Because I offer a bigger challenge than slipping in under the radar in the dead of night. I offer a bigger challenge than avoiding the DEA and merciless Colombian cocaine dealers. I offer nothing less than the reshaping of the world! There are no missiles on *this* chopper, just minicams. And no corner of this Perfect World escapes my floating eye!

Past, present, future—all are laid out for me now. This is *Time Chopper Twelve*, a unique new concept in televised entertainment. Here in the heavens, I buzz and float. I bring my sarcastic message to a nation weary of double-talk, a nation weary of persuasion techniques and opinion polls. Billboards across America proclaim AMERICA SAYS YES WHEN IAN SAYS NO! Crowds gather in city parks to do the Wave and chant my name. A grateful nation throws away its footballs! Softball and basketball games do not dissolve in stupid arguments! Dogs bark my name in Morse code. The faint shouts of women reach me as a distant whisper: "Ian, my Ian . . ."

Up we go, past the tall buildings, up in the amazingly silent chopper, no louder than a cat's purr, up to the boring stars, to the very edge of the depleted ozone layer. Below me, I see an America that wants me to invade their lives. I see an America that wants me to televise. Over the hum of the discreet engines, pockets of America think of me and sigh. *Big* pockets.

And I'm on the cellular phone, talking on all five lines at once, counting hundred-dollar bills in the sleek aluminum basket beside me. I will not be bored! In *Time Chopper Twelve* I can cross Time like the same river twice! My teeth are straight and white, any minor personality defects smoothed over like a lump on a runway, my body lithe and muscular. My masseuse, Helga, kneads my powerful shoulders as I sit in my skybound Barcalounger. I'm making lists, checking them twice.

There's my executive secretary on Line Three: "We've got a problem," she says. "Re your ban on teddy bears. A coalition of three-year-olds is marching on Washington, oh wealthy one. Right now they're holding a teddy-bear protest in front of the White House."

"What about the Presidents?" I ask.

"Bob and Ray won't issue a statement," she says. "But the toddlers say that until they get their teddy bears back, they're going to stage a red, white, and blue demonstration. A third of them are going to turn red with rage, a third white from weeping, and the final third are going to hold their breath until they turn blue. Christo, the artist, is attaching them all at the waist with Velcro and covering them with gauze. The whole thing is being photographed by Avedon for a special issue of *Vanity Fair*, with photo captions by Chris Buckley. Can you afford this negative publicity, oh righteous one?"

"Oh, let the kids have their damn teddy bears," I say. "I guess there's a lot of things I don't like that I'm glad are around."

"Like what, oh sneermeister?"

"Like Paul Harvey, thrash rock, cars, telephones, underwater photography—hello? Hello?"

She'd hung up on me, no doubt to deal with this crisis.

We're passing over the prison. This is where everyone who has ever wronged me faces his or her eternal punishment. First-time offenders are made judges on "Star Search." Second-time offenders are made competitors on "Star Search." I take mercy on third-time offenders and give them all jobs as spokesmodels on the Shoales Television Network, where they are extremely well-paid for doing nothing, and are frequently interviewed by *People* magazine!

"What a guy," says Sarge around his cigar.

There's the Republicans on Line One, the Democrats on Line Two. "Run," they beg me. "Run." I laugh into the receiver. President? Me? Where's the power in that? Where's the glory?

"Hold all calls," I bark.

"Yes, your grumpiness. Your wish is our command, oh bitter one."

My valet mixes me a smoothie as my personal assistant hands me a list of stupidities to be righted. Yes, we will traverse space and time in this amazing spacious machine and correct what is wrong everywhere. We will tear down the stupid and build up the smart!

But first, to keep me humble (humility doesn't come easy when you're the wisest guy who ever drew breath), let's point this thing at the past. We must glimpse my pathetic old self. We set the course for Los Angeles, 1987, to an adults-only apartment complex (what a quaint concept, so old-fashioned, so outmoded). We dolly in to a set of drawn shades. Special devices pull those shades back, and Minicam Seven pulls in for a close-up of my past self, asleep. The machinery of memory is switched to On. I remember this day well. It was perhaps the worst day of my life. It's ten minutes after seven. The alarm is about to go off in the eighties, that most horrible and stupid of decades. We will not interrupt the troubled sleep of our hero, myself. He is besieged enough, poor fellow!

All across America hostile forces are picking up the telephone to bring him bad news. All across America unfriendly hands file papers against him. His name figures prominently in bathroom graffiti in ladies' rooms across the land. In a hut in Haiti the visage of Ian Shoales is subjected to hideous punishments. A photograph of Ian Shoales is being examined by Mr. Phelps, who is assembling the Impossible Missions Force to destroy him, forever. In Moscow, special agents of the KGB are being dispatched to America, just to silence his voice. A madman's cold finger is poised on a deadly machine.

And poor Ian is his own worst enemy. He is tortured by his own thoughts. As Wo Fat to McGarrett, Blofeld to Bond, THRUSH to U.N.C.L.E., Klingons to the Federation, Moriarty to Holmes, Corday to Marat, Gradus to Shade, Roman to Celt, Barbarian to Rome, the World to Lebanon, Sitting Bull to Custer, Boer to Black, Ernie to Bert, Santa Anna to Crockett, Wellington to Napoleon, Cobra to Joe, so are Ian's thoughts to Ian. He sleeps on, anathematized!

No. We will not wake poor Ian. But we *will* enter his teeming brain. We're going to keep the chopper hovering here for the entire *length of the book!* Sure, it's an expensive shot, and the telepathic microcams prone to mechanical failure, and my contempt for ESP a serious barrier to mind reading, but if Spielberg or Cimino can waste millions, so can I. You know why? Because *I'm the richest man in the world*.

"Turn on the cloak of invisibility, Sarge."

"Aye aye, oh he who sleeps late in the morning."

There's the alarm. God, that's loud. That's so annoying. It must be waking up the neighbors. But still Ian doesn't stir. The neighbors are pounding on the walls, begging Ian to turn it off. There! He tosses! He grumbles! He is on the brink of his greatest despair! His greatest success! If you could only see me here, Ian, if you could only know what the future has in store. Hit the snooze bar, Ian. Dream.

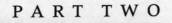

PART TWO

*M*orning

in which we pursue the fame and fortune
denied us so long

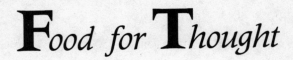

Food for Thought

Consciousness is not a plaything.

—R. D. Laing

O Lord. Congress relieve me.

—last words of Meriwether Lewis

down the rabbit hole

Is that my voice? Oh. Answering machine:

You've tried to reach me, Ian Shoales,
But you've reached a machine.
Think of all the wires and poles
That led up to this scene.
I don't want to talk to you.
In fact I'm fast asleep.
So what you got to say to me,
Say it at the beep.

Beep. Another voice: "Is this the number to call for the Patti Page records? Hello? I want to order the Patti Page records. I don't really have a major credit card—"

"No major credit card?" I shouted. "You got no major credit card? You might as well kill yourself right now."

"Hello? Patti Page?"

I threw a pillow at the answering machine. Check out this amazing feature: it stopped. The digital clock said seven: ten. Time: first step to fascism. Somebody's painted WAKE UP on the wall. Ha. That cuts no ice with me, pal. You'll have to do better than that. You got to get up pretty early in the morning to get *me* up pretty early in the morning. Get up for what? Oh right. Job. Money. Let me just close my eyes a second here, and think about the implications.

If I could just get the money without the work, that would be the Perfect Job. The Perfect Job Application: *Who are you?* "Shoales, Ian." *Congratulations! Would you like a raise?* Give me the Perfect Credit Application: *Have you ever owned anything?* "Nope." *That's okay. Here's your card, sir!* Maybe I could have actually earned a degree after my ten years of college if I'd taken the Perfect Final Exam: *Name as much as you can remember about this subject, or, if you*

*can't remember anything about that, name as much as you can remember
about last night. Or anything. You have the rest of your life to finish this
test. Begin now.*

School days. I still have those stupid dreams: alarm goes off,
I'm late for a test I've never heard of for a class I didn't know I had,
I rush out the door, realize I don't have any clothes on, stuck downtown with no clothes on—everybody has that dream, those stupid
naked dreams. What's that tapping?

"Ian? Mr. Shoales?"

Somebody was tapping lightly at the window.

I staggered out of the rich man's bed and lurched to the window, hoisted up the Levelors. A handsome silver-haired man in a
blue three-piece suit was standing in the flower bed. He looked like
a slightly overweight John DeLorean.

"Good morning," he whispered. "I'm Alan Wilcox, CEO of
ProCorGenTel. I hate to disturb you at this hour—"

A leisurely snap of the wrist revealed his Rolex, which disappeared up his sleeve as fast as it appeared.

"—but it's time to go to work. I'll give you a few minutes to
get dressed. We have a nice hot breakfast waiting in the limo."

I threw on my rumpled sharkskin suit, my least dirty shirt, my
least bilious green tie. I trotted curbside.

"I hope sausages are all right," he said, opening the door. "I
have them ground especially for me. And I assume you take your
eggs over easy."

"Fine," I said. A small stove jutted from the rear of the front
seat, next to a television monitor which seemed to be changing
stations every five seconds or so. I settled back in the patented leather
substitute.

"This is Sarge, the driver," he said.

"Hiya Mac," said Sarge.

"Coffee?" said the CEO. "It's Colombian."

"Try the orange juice," said Sarge. "I squeezed the oranges
myself."

"Delicious," I said. "What's the job?"

"Oh," he said, waving a hand. "Filing. Answering phones."

"I'm not very good with telephones," I said. "I tend to get
rude."

"You don't *have* to answer them," he said hastily. "You don't even have to file if you don't want to. I don't care." He loosened his tie and sighed. "I just don't care anymore."

Traffic around us was moving slowly. Porsches and BMWs were vague shapes through the tinted glass, like steel dolphins in dirty water.

"Look at that sun coming up," he said. "I can't appreciate that. I can see it, but I can't appreciate it. I'm too damn busy."

"That's not the sun, sir," said Sarge. "That's a billboard. For a wine cooler."

"I can't even tell the difference anymore," said Mr. Wilcox.

"You should take some time off, Mr. Wilcox," I suggested.

"Call me Alan," he said. "They called me Wilkie at Harvard," he added wistfully.

"I never went to Harvard," I said.

"I went to Yale Drama School," said Sarge.

"You can call me Wilkie anyway," said Alan. "Both of you. Those were the days. Look at that sun. Is *that* the sun, Sarge?"

"Yes sir," said Sarge. "I mean Wilkie."

"You know," he said, "I was having lunch the other day with Bert Colfax of Mingo UniCorp. He was telling me how much stock we needed for a leveraged buyout of ComFaxCompuComCom. We'd agreed on everything but what we were going to call the new company. Syncresis? Serendipicon? Synchronicitis? We couldn't agree to agree, and by the time we did agree on a name, ComFax-CompuComCom had already merged with PetroBoBoDollarSine, changed their name to RoboPhobix, bought Brazil, and declared bankruptcy. They made a *killing* while we were watching our Perrier go flat. I've lost the edge, boys. I've lost the edge." He sighed again, and slumped in the seat.

"Excuse me," I said, "um, Wilkie, but is there a point to this?"

"No," he said. "Thank God, no. Have some more coffee. Have as much as you want. It's a write-off."

"What exactly do you want from me?" I asked.

"I don't know," said Wilkie. "A reason to live, maybe? I was just going to send the limo for you, but then I thought I'd tag along. I take your commentaries to heart, you know. I keep a journal. I write down everything you say that applies to my life, and try my best to live by your moral code."

"Great," I said.

"Do you remember the commentary you did called 'Corporate Man'?"

"Sure," I said. "But our readers might not, so let's take a look at it now, shall we?"

Wilkie obliged by opening his journal. There, in his forceful hand, we read the following transcription:

op/ed from ian

"Corporate Man"

The corporate man: Ted Turner, Rupert Murdoch, Howard Hughes, Lee Iacocca, Blake Carrington, Donald Trump, the iron god of Ayn Rand, the distinguished air, the silver hair. He's the man in search of excellence. He's the man who takes his pleasure where he finds it. He's got two hundred blue suits, he's the man with the cellular phone.

He calls his driver by his first name. He's got a whirl-pool in the trunk of the limo. He drives his Ferrari full throttle on full-moon nights; he takes the dark corners with a tiny squeal. He could fly a helicopter if he had to; he never has to. He's got regal trappings. His trousers from Hong Kong have a crease so sharp you could cut yourself if you got that close, but you can't. He's sur-rounded by prizefighters and mercenaries, former CIA, Uzis under jackets. He's surrounded by twenty Mormons, a briefcase chained to each wrist.

He's got a Lucite desk with nothing on it but a red telephone, a desk the size of Delaware, a yacht, a Jamaican secretary. He's got Italian sunglasses that change shades with the shifting of light.

If he has a wife she shops with Nancy Reagan. If he has a mistress, she's a former international fashion model. He gives her a gay bodyguard and has her followed by a lawyer with a drinking problem. He wears provocative cologne. If he can't order in French, he'll bring a man who can. He has a standing reservation at a restaurant whose name you wouldn't recognize if you heard it.

He looks *great* on television. He is a master of the persuasion technique called "bluntness." He points a finger at the camera and says, "I built this company with the sweat of other people's brow. I sat in the boardroom in the stink of Cuban cigars and the flop sweat of the three-piece losers, and then I pounced. This is mine, America, but you can have a piece of it. What do you want? A car? A razor blade? A computer peripheral? A stock option? It's all mine, but you can have some." And who doesn't want a piece of a hardball dreamer?

He turned the company around! Heads turn when he walks into a room! He has elusive principles written in invisible ink in a book locked away in a private vault. He will never run for President, no never, no never, he will never have a tattoo, he won't take your lip, he can handle your jive, he knows the bottom line, he knows baloney when he hears it, he doesn't mince words. He's a walking merger, he's a public relations stroke, a line in the Society column, the cover of *Business Week*. He strokes the corporate image till it purrs. He's the friendliest hostile takeover in the world. He's so diversified, he's *everything*. He's the wolf at the door, the pirate with a briefcase, the man who found the pot of gold.

But under the golf tan, the tan of the poolside phone call, the pressure is rising. He's got everything to lose, he's got the world to gain. Paris, New York, London, L.A.! He's got a chartered jet to whisk him away from whispers against him. He can't sleep because men exactly like him want what he has. He doesn't want to sleep, he's the king of the corporate kingdom. What good is sleep? Sleep costs money. The king can never sleep, never die, he can only resign.

He's the modern hero. We want him to go on forever, or, if he falls, we want it all to fall with him. For there is no dynasty, no family, no progeny to continue the reign. The corporation is the family, and when it gets tired of Daddy, Daddy's gotta go. Bye-bye, Daddy. The strong hand quivers, but the Swiss watch ticks on. The stride may falter, but the Italian shoes will last forever. The deposed king lives out the post-corporate blues: adviser to Presidents, a brainstorm in a think tank, the financial expert on the evening news, the well-placed source. He's a double-dipping golden parachute, hefting his irons on the links.

And finally the burst vessel. The terse paragraph in *Time*. Ashes in a silver urn. There are the remains: the dust of a lonely man, who gave his life for power, then power passed him by. I gotta go.

and now back to our story

"That moved me," said Wilkie, shutting his journal. "Just think. It took a sarcastic wise-ass loser with no visible means of support to turn my head around, value-wise."

"Well thanks," I said. "What does your company make anyway?"

"Deals," he said. "I really don't know exactly. I just want to play golf. I know you hate golf."

"It'd be a pleasant walk if you didn't have to carry those stupid clubs around."

"But I hope you won't begrudge me the sole pleasure of my greedy useless life?"

"Oh not at all," I said.

"Isn't he forceful?" Wilkie asked the driver.

"Sure," said Sarge.

"And this is my parking space," said Wilkie, as we pulled into the sun-splashed lot. "See? There's my name written on an oblong piece of concrete. One might as well engrave one's name on the shifting sands."

"Very well put, sir," said Sarge.

36

"The hell with it," said Wilkie. "Let's face facts. I'm burned out. I *want* out. Trouble is, who can fill my shoes? Who can take over this damn thing?" He turned to Sarge. "*You* don't want the damn thing."

"*Keep* the damn thing," said Sarge.

"I dread going up there," said Wilkie. "But who wants the company?"

"Wait a minute," said Sarge. "What about Ian?"

"Why didn't *I* think of that?" said Wilkie, slapping his forehead. "You'd be Perfect. What do you say? Want to be CEO of a major corporation?"

"I guess," I said. "Can I paint my name over yours on that slab of concrete?"

He waved a hand. "It's settled then," he said. "Great. Now I can disappear. My only desire now is to become an anonymous seeker after small pleasures."

"You like fishing, sir?" said Sarge.

"I've never fished," said Wilkie, his voice cracking.

"I know where the big ones bite," said Sarge.

"Can I get out of the car now?" I asked.

"Cards," said Wilkie. "I used to play cards. I *love* to play cards."

"Nothing's holding you back now, sir," said Sarge.

"Is it okay to get out of the car?" I asked.

"The kids are grown," said Wilkie. "My wife left me five years ago."

"My kids too," said Sarge. "And my ex just wants money."

"Yoo hoo," I said.

"Yes," said Wilkie. "In these litigious times the failure of love often leads to cash transactions."

"You should try your hand at writing, sir," said Sarge.

"I could write a book," said Wilkie.

"Oh yeah," I said. "That's what the world needs. Another ghost-written piece of self-congratulatory crap that pretends to be a formula for success but is actually just another lamebrain fantasy for overweight losers stuck halfway up the corporate ladder. No offense."

"Actually I was thinking more of a novel," he said.

"About fishing?" said Sarge.

"Hmmmm," said Wilkie, removing his tie.

"Successful people don't read," I said. "They skim."

"So where should we go?" said Sarge.

"Montana?" said Wilkie. "I've always wanted to see Montana."

"Montana," whispered Sarge.

"Are they expecting me up there?" I asked. "Hello?"

"What?" said Wilkie. "Oh yeah. They know somebody's coming. Good luck."

"We could get a cabin—" said Sarge. I slammed the door on his voice, annoyed. They were going on vacation, for God's sake, and here I was, stuck with a goddam corporation. I took the private elevator up. A team of secretaries stood up and applauded when I entered the foyer.

"Things are going to change around here," I snarled. They all cheered. "I want a top-of-the-line stereo system and thirty color televisions brought in. I need Beta, VHS, and two half-inch VCRs. I want a Barcalounger molded to fit my body."

A dead ringer for Mary Tyler Moore strode forward and stooped to measure my inseam. I *liked* that. I said, "I want a series of blank checks, a computer, current issues of every magazine, every book ever written, and a team of experts in my office *immediately*." I stopped and thought for a minute. "I want to find the woman who sat next to me in my Myth and Modern Culture class back in 1972— you know, the one who stopped me after class to tell me I reminded her of Palamon in the Knight's Tale from *Canterbury Tales*. And bring me a copy of Chaucer so I can find out if I'm flattered or not. Matter of fact, is there any kind of time machine in the building?"

"We can find one, sir," enthused a woman, a startling lookalike for Judy in the Time/Life Books commercial (Aviation Series).

"What's your name?" I demanded.

"Judy," she said.

"Give yourself a raise!" I shouted. "You all get raises!"

"Hurrah!" they shouted.

"Install a satellite dish on the roof, and launch a satellite immediately. I want inventors, I want ordinary people brought into my office. I want a porch fitted to the outside of the building. And a barbecue grill. And a pitcher of cold lemonade. And a list of our corporate assets. What the hell—give yourselves another raise!"

"Oh boy!" they shouted.

"Wait a minute," I said. "Let's make that *equal partners!*"

"Yay," said Judy. "Can we turn the foyer into a daycare?"

"Yes!" I said. "And take off those high heels!"

Forty uncomfortable shoes went flying in the air.

"From now on you can wear anything you want," I said. "And if there's no work for you to do, don't try to look busy. *I hate that.*"

"Can I read a magazine?"

"Yes."

"How about workshops? Can we have seminars and feminist support groups?"

"No problem."

"Can we install a steam bath and Jacuzzi?"

"I don't see why not," I said. "I'm going to my office."

I strode into the office and sat down behind the huge desk. A secretary followed me in and lay down in front of me.

"Take me, Ian!" she said.

"Nuts to that, ma'am," I said. "Until night falls, this is a family book, strictly PG-13. I want this thing to be more than mere evidence for a Meese Commission. You want to meet me when the book's over, great. But I'm not gonna share my sexual fantasies with the reading public, unless there's a point to be made."

"What a guy," she said, leaving. Another woman stuck her head through the door.

"My name's Yvonne. I love you," she said. Somewhat halfheartedly, I thought, considering whose book, after all, this was.

I sat behind my immense desk, making random rude phone calls, while burly workmen installed television screens all about me. When the Barcalounger arrived, I leaped into it. I had a lot of thinking to do. I was in control of my life at last, and it was hard work. I needed to rest. I closed my weary eyes, then opened them slightly to experience an odd little hallucination. First I could hear the buzzing of a distant alarm. *Probably a car alarm,* I thought, *somebody's MG getting relieved of its Blaupunkt, yay. Stolen music, that's all it is. Maybe a smoke alarm? A stalled elevator? It's got nothing to do with me.*

And I imagined that I wasn't in a corporate office, but in a bed somewhere. Television on. Blinds closed. I could see the writing on the wall: WAKE UP. *Interesting how dreams work. Damn that buzzing. Ignore it. Hit the snooze bar, I mean the intercom.*

"I want the world on this desk," I barked. "And I want it *now!*"

One of my secretaries stormed in. "I'm Barb," she said. "Look, I know you've got committees meeting all over the building. I know you've got a staff of researchers trying to track down Captain Nemo and Judge Crater. You're getting close to the truth about the Lindbergh baby and who killed Kennedy. You're dancing on the edge of the space/time continuum, going back and forth through time and space with this book of yours, and I appreciate the effort, I do, but this Utopia just isn't working for me. It's too one-sided."

"Listen Barb." I yawned. "Every Perfect World is based on exclusion. An autocracy is Perfect if you're an autocrat. It's a closed system."

"But where are the clothes, Ian? Where's the shopping? I don't want to dress like your fantasy."

"But you look great in that nurse outfit."

"Ian, you're not even my type. You just don't interest me sexually. You barely interest me as a human being. Ian, you have to accept the fact that you're a jerk."

"Oh duh," I said. "Tell me something I don't know."

"What happened to *Mask*? I was going to curl up with a cup of Nestle's tonight and watch it, but I can't find it on videocassette anywhere. It's as if every print of that movie has vanished from the face of the earth. And *Cousin Cousine*. *Every* French movie is gone except *Shoot the Piano Player, Weekend, Going Places,* and *Breathless.* You could have at least saved the Richard Gere version."

"At least I saved Richard Gere. I got him teaching male-sensitivity workshops in federal prisons."

"Fat lot of good that does me. Look, is my pleasure in life supposed to be diminished just because you don't like what I like?"

"Okay, okay, we'll put something in the book that *you* like. What do you want? A carrot cake recipe? A Chippendale's calendar? Want me to pose in bikini briefs with a little bowtie? Is America ready for that? I think not, frankly."

"You've got to make your point of view clear, Ian. You've got to give people something they can get a handle on. They've got to understand you."

"What? Was I mincing words?"

"Ten-best lists, Ian. *Esquire* does it. 'Entertainment Tonight' does it. Every critic does it."

"How am I gonna find ten of *anything* I like? Besides, I hate ten-best lists. They're shorthand for the bright, and guideposts for the stupid."

"Do you want this book to sell or not?"

your top ten countdown

top ten rentals to avoid on a first video-date

1. *Corpse Grinders* She won't like it, believe me.

2. *A Man and a Woman* He won't like it, believe me.

3. *Rocky Horror Picture Show* This is the least hip date in America.

4. *The Way We Were* Overused first-date material.

5. *Dawn of the Dead* Save this one till you know each other better.

6. *Freaks* There's something about this Ted Browning classic that will lead a woman to hate you and everything you stand for. After seeing this movie with you, she will call your parents and request that you be put someplace where you will be of no further harm to yourself or others.

7. *Every Woman Has a Fantasy* Contrary to what you may hear from desperate pornographers, pornography is not designed to enhance a couple's pleasure. Pornography is designed to make a lonely man forget his loneliness.

8. *Eraserhead* Save this one for the birth of your first-born. Just *kidding, God,* you're so *sensitive.*

9. *Blue Velvet* I use this movie the way some people use astrology—as a compatibility indicator. If you're a fan of *Blue Velvet,* affinity is possible between us. This is not first-date material; this is the acid test for a long haul.

10. ***The Gods Must Be Crazy*** On a first date? Come on, use a little imagination for crying out loud. And don't buy those little dinky cups of Italian ice cream either.

This is kind of fun! Let's try another one.

your top ten countdown
top ten recurring events many Americans take to their bosoms but whose appeal just baffles the hell out of me

1. ***Super Bowl*** Unnatural body movement to attain silly results.

2. ***Ballet*** Same deal.

3. ***Opera*** Silly plots and unnatural voices.

4. ***Broadway Shows*** Broadway is a bright museum for dead plays, or plays that imitate dead plays, plays that trot out epiphanies like dance numbers, and dance numbers like shopworn epiphanies. All this at a ticket price more than most people make in a week.

5. ***Situation Comedies*** Bill Cosby buys a Cuisinart. Then the fun begins.

6. ***Masterpiece Theatre*** Television for people who hate television. With that built-in snob appeal, it doesn't need to be entertaining.

7. ***Sylvester Stallone Movies*** This guy's no Chuck Norris.

8. ***Performance Art*** Music loops instead of melodies. Unconnected images. Lazy playwriting. Dance by non-dancers. Frequently employs nudity, however, which means it beats Broadway. But not by much.

9. *Lotteries*   Luck gets a bureaucracy.

10. *Top Ten Lists*   These things sure are addictive though. Once you get started making them, it's hard to st—

perfect strangers

Someone was tugging at my sleeve again.

"What *is* it, Barb?" I asked, cramming lists into my pockets.

"We've got those reports you wanted," she said. "Here's the woman who sat next to you in your Mythology class."

I took the file from her. The tab said simply RUTH.

"And here's the list of corporate assets," she said, handing me a single piece of paper laminated in see-through red plastic. In the upper left-hand corner, I noted the ProCorGenTel logo—a snake eating its own tail.

Neatly centered in the middle of the page, it read:

WHAT WE GOT

CONVERGENCE AIRLINES: "Arise & Fly!"

NEW FOOD GROCERIES: "New Food for a New You!"

L'HOTEL ENNUI: "Where Languor Rules."
    Los Angeles, New York, Boston, Paris, Miami, London, Nassau, Moscow (North Dakota).

BUNNIBANK: "Where Bucks Breed"

DESTINY ENTERTAINMENTS: "We Make the Food of Love"
    Records & Tapes
    Audio/Visual
    Artist Management
    Research & Development (Front for Top-Secret Government Operations)

"And," Barb said, "Mr. Wilcox wanted you to take a look at this."

She handed me a palm-sized rectangular object.

"It's something R & D has been working on. Wilkie said he couldn't think of anybody who'd enjoy it more."

I gave the object the once-over. It seemed to be some kind of remote-control device. At the top of the unit it said DESTINY COMMANDER. I pointed it at the bank of television screens and pressed a button. Thirty screens leaped into life.

"Good morning, Mr. Shoales," came a smooth pleasant voice. This thingie could talk! It sounded rather like Burgess Meredith. "What you see on the monitors is just the tip of the iceberg of my capabilities. Let me slide back my protective panel to display my full range."

All right, I thought. *This is the life.*

It began to vibrate in my hand, and the front of the unit slid back to reveal *another* set of controls. A thin aerial telescoped upwards from its surface.

"Use the platinum stylus to depress the pads," said Destiny Commander. "The System Selecter will now appear on the liquid crystal display. A powerful Zeitgeist lens is provided in the rear of the unit for easier viewing—"

"Excuse me," Barb said. "There are three men to see you."

"I don't want to see anybody," I said.

"They have guns," she said.

"Send them in," I said.

I shoved the files and Destiny Commander into a desk drawer. No sooner had I shut the drawer than the oak door bust into splinters and three men stepped across the rubble. Two of them held smoking machine guns.

"Sorry about the door," the man on the left said insincerely. He dropped a clip on the floor, and put in another, aiming the bore at the ceiling.

"It was open," I said.

"So are sewers," he sneered. I shut my mouth and looked them over. The two guys with the machine guns were my age: a young Henry Silva, a tall Dane Clark. They wore sharkskin suits—better-pressed than mine—with little porkpie hats and wraparound mirrored shades. They looked like hit men from some Frank Sinatra movie, circa 1962. They looked *sharp.*

And the third man? The man in the middle? He was Wilkie's chauffeur, Sarge. But gone was his friendly demeanor, and gone was his chauffeur's cap. He nodded his head at me, grimly, then unbuttoned his coat and loosened his belt. Immediately his stomach began to overflow his waistline. His whole body began to bulge outward, like a balloon slowly filing with water. The two gunmen screwed up their faces and looked away.

"Excuse me while I change into someone more comfortable," said Sarge, his voice changing as he expanded. There was a rip of stitches. His Sansabelt snapped with a crack. "I saw Mr. Wilcox off on the nine o'clock flight to Helena, Montana," he said. "That removes one obstacle to my takeover plans, and leaves only you."

The last of his uniform lay in shreds on the floor. He now stood before me, an immensely fat man (I know, I know, you're saying, "Come on, Ian, another sinister fat man? Haven't you seen *Maltese Falcon*? Haven't you read *Woman in White*? Aren't you familiar with the James Bond oeuvre?" I can only say, "Hey, this *really happened*, okay? Would I make something like this up? An expanding fat man? Give me a break, folks.") wearing a very well-cut ice-cream suit that fit him like a glove or, more precisely, a mitten. He donned a Panama hat, doffed it, and snapped his fingers.

The gunner on his left went back through the smoking doorway and came back with a briefcase. He handed the briefcase to the second gunner who opened it, removed a file folder, and handed the file folder to the fat man, who had been standing all this time regarding me with an air of amused and dismissive malignance. (This is a *hard* thing to do. The longest I've been able to assume an air of amused and dismissive malignance is eleven point five seconds, and I've had practice.) When the folder was in the fat man's hands, he opened it, and read aloud.

"Shoales, Ian," he intoned in the kind of voice you'd expect a sinister fat man to have. " '1953. Stole picture of Roy Rogers from the lunch pail of little curly-haired girl in kindergarten class. 1955. Pushed Wayne Huey into the duck pond. 1956. Used crib sheets to win the spelling bee.' " He looked up from his reading. "I'm just hitting the high points, Mr. Shoales, we don't have time for details."

I nodded and listened.

" 'Underage drinking. Fornication. Illegal drug use. Refusal to get haircut at insistence of assistant principal. Libelous statements. Lying to parents. Lying to girlfriends.' "

"Excuse me for asking," I interrupted, "but what the hell is this?"

"Why Mr. Shoales," said the fat man with a wintry smile. "I thought you knew. This is your Permanent Record. You must have known it would come back to haunt you."

"Okay," I said. "What's the gag?"

"This *is* a hostile takeover, Mr. Shoales," he said. "I hope you'll go quietly, and we won't be forced to make any of this public."

"Let me get this straight," I said. "I have to decide whether the power and stature of running a major corporation are worth the embarrassment of, say, having my father discover that I stole part of his coin collection in 1967 so I could see Dana Andrews in *Hot Rods from Hell*?"

The Fat Man nodded.

"And if I decide it *is* worth it? After all, my reputation couldn't really sink much lower."

"We have other incentives."

"Such as?"

"Such as this!" said the machiner gunner on his right. He cut loose with a burst that typed the corporate logo high on the wall, and another that made my wall of video screens explode in a shattering haze. "The next one will be through your guts!"

"I was thinking more in terms of a cash settlement," I said.

"Oh," said the machine gunner.

"You know," I said. "Severance pay."

"You surprise me, sir," said the Fat Man. "Your business acumen is astonishing, considering your lack of experience. You drive a hard bargain. I had hoped to avoid this, but—"

He snapped his fingers. Each machine gunner handed him a check, which he handed to me.

"This," he said, "is a nine-billion-dollar settlement. You'll notice that it's a number so big it took two checks to write it. Nine billion is the number decided upon by the stockholders. There is no negotiation."

"Thank you, Mr. Anthony," I said, accepting the checks. "And thank Mr. Tipton for me too."

"References to an old television show," I explained at their puzzled looks, as I reached for the files in my drawer. " 'The Millionaire.' Many episodes were directed by the young Robert Altman." My hands closed around the remote-control device.

"Your mind is filled with useless information," said the Fat Man.

I shrugged and put my hands in my pockets, thus safely spiriting the Destiny Commander away. I'd earned it. Who in America could appreciate it more? With it and nine billion dollars a fellow could live on Easy Street for *months*.

"If you're through cleaning out your desk, Mr. Burst and Mr. Sunder will escort you back to your residence." The Fat Man gestured, and Burst and Sunder fell in beside me.

As they marched me back through the foyer, now crowded with toddlers and aerobics instructors, the secretaries saluted. It had been a noble effort. I met each misty eye, waved away the half-formed words of farewell.

"We'll miss you, Ian," said Judy.

"Thanks," I said. I didn't lose control. It hadn't been a failure, not at all, just another nine-billion-dollar mistake. It happens all the time. It happens every day.

"Move it," said Burst. Clutching the file folder marked RUTH, I stepped into the private elevator, and we all went down.

perfect crime

I was having trouble telling these guys apart. Mr. Burst was driving, I think. Mr. Sunder kept me covered.

"What kind of gun is that?" I asked, trying to break the ice.

"This?" said Mr. Sunder, smiling. "This is the Wilmington SXZ 9000 Model 47. It has no more heft than a Fanner .50, and looks like an ordinary staple gun."

"Do you mind," I asked casually, "if I take a look at it?"

"Sure," he said, handing it to me.

"Don't move," I said, pointing the thing at him.

"Damn!" he said, snapping his fingers. "I should have known better than to trust you."

"Pull over!" I said to the driver.

His eyes met mine in the rearview mirror.

"That's not the Wilmington SXZ," said Mr. Burst.

"What is it then, smart guy?" I asked.

"A staple gun," he said. "The upholstery was coming loose."

"Where's the SXZ?" said Mr. Sunder.

"I dunno," said Mr. Burst. "Check under the seat."

I threw down the staple gun and sighed. "Jeeze," I said. "What'll they think of next?"

Mr. Burst said, "The Frellington people are coming up with a semiautomatic weapon so small you have to use tweezers to fire it."

"Here it is," said Mr. Sunder. "No, wait, that's a coat hanger."

"And the Japanese," said Mr. Burst, "got a digital job that straps to your wrist and doubles as a calculator. You gotta be real careful what mode you're in, though. I heard some guys were splitting up a lunch tab and blew away the maitre d'."

"That kind of thing will happen more and more now that the feds took away the business-lunch deduction," I said.

"The hell with it," said Mr. Sunder, giving up the search. "We weren't going to kill him till we stopped anyway."

"Don't tell him, for Christ sake," said Mr. Burst.

"Oh right," he said. "Sorry." He looked at me. "Sorry."

"What happened to the good old Uzi?" I asked.

"That's for terrorists," scoffed Mr. Burst.

"Cocaine dealers," said Mr. Sunder. "Professional hit men."

"Oh," I inquired politely, "and what are you guys?"

"This is just part-time," said Mr. Burst. "Once I pass the bar exam, I'm waving bye-bye to this."

"I have an MBA from Harvard Business School," said Mr. Sunder. "I'm just climbing the old ladder rung by rung."

"And which rung is this?" I asked.

Mr. Sunder started chewing his fingernails nervously. "How'd you come to own a major corporation anyway?"

"That's a long story," I said. "But basically it came to me

through my fame and talent as a nationally respected social critic."

"Get out of here," said Mr. Burst.

"Go on," said Mr. Sunder, his voice slightly muffled by the seat cushion. "I got it!" He emerged holding a pocket calculator.

"Careful with that thing," I said.

"This isn't it," he said. "Damn. We've *gotta* find it. We've just *gotta*, or the boys in the stockroom will file a report."

"And just what do you criticize, smart guy?" asked Mr. Burst.

"You know," I said. "America. Television."

"How come I've never heard of you?" asked Mr. Sunder.

"You have to pay attention. All you guys read is *The Wall Street Journal* and *Soldier of Fortune*."

"That's not true!" said Mr. Sunder. "We pay attention."

"We watch 'L.A. Law,' " said Mr. Burst.

"There's more to life than 'L.A. Law,' " I said.

"I doubt it," said Mr. Sunder. "Here we are."

We'd pulled up in front of the apartment complex again.

"Okay," said Mr. Burst with a sigh. "We'll use my gun. What we're going to do is put a bullet in the back of your head, and leave you on the steps as a warning to others."

"What others?" I asked.

"Never mind that," said Mr. Burst. "Just hand those checks over to Mr. Sunder."

"Hold it," I said. I half-stood up, and took the SXZ from the seat beneath me. I'd thought it was a seat buckle until I realized I was wearing my seat belt.

"Put your hands on top of your heads," I said.

"I hope I pass my bar exam soon," said Mr. Burst, complying. "I'm getting slow."

"Give me that staple gun," I said.

"Now how can I do that?" said Mr. Sunder. "I've got my hands on top of my head."

I reached over and took it. Covering them with one hand, I shoved the staple gun and the RUTH file into my waistband and got out of the car.

"By the time you get back it will be too late to stop payment on these checks," I said. "So I'm going to let you live."

"Thanks," said Mr. Sunder.

"Now get out of here," I said.

"How can I drive with my hands on my head?" said Mr. Burst.

"You can take them down now," I said.

"Thanks," he said.

"For nothing," sneered Mr. Sunder.

As they peeled out I sent a burst over their heads to speed them on their way. A shower of silver sprinkled down and fell with a light tinkle between me and the cloud of dust raised by their retreat. Little shards of silver lay in the driveway. I stopped to check them out: staples. Damn, these weapons were hard to tell apart. I threw away the machine gun, tucked the stapler back in my pants. It was almost ten o'clock. By the time I reached Hollywood Boulevard the banks would be open. I began to walk down the driveway. As I walked, I opened the folder labeled RUTH and began to read.

perfect woman

This is top secret, your eyes only, shred and destroy, memorize and retain. All the resources of this mighty corporation were brought to bear upon the subject Ruth, not her real name.

When she was born under a moon as bright as a lucky dollar, the doctor smiled a gold-tooth smile and all the nurses sighed. Her daddy loved her dearly, and her mama blessed her genes with a clear true voice. Ruth grew up singing. Her toes knew the bark of the neighborhood trees. Yes, she had dollies, and yes, there were boys, but it was movies and books that charged her life. She lost herself in ivory pages, faded stories. She could see in the violence and color of movies a stillness and soothing presence. Why does America love the movies? Like a baby, Ruth knew, America sings itself to sleep.

Even in her voluptuous adulthood, despite the blows and old flames, there remained within her the spark of that little girl who sat by a cold window on a winter night, reading *David Copperfield*; she watched the snow flurries in the spill of downstairs light, and heard below her parents and friends drink, and sing the old songs.

Ruth, we find, is either a fallen angel or a mortal half-way risen, trapped between earth and air. Her album, *Stone & Sky*, is still played on rare FM stations. Any rainy three A.M. turn the dial to find her. Listen for a steely alto with a bending growl. Listen for blue notes and blue themes. Listen for the teeth of a broken heart. She sings clear-eyed fantasies of refuge. She makes you feel the way a werewolf on the verge of change might feel, and wish you owned the moon.

Her brown hair is careless, her brown eyes careful and large, her lips full of care, as wide and pale as a strip of beach glimpsed by air in moonlight. Her large white teeth show often, and she doesn't take a smile back if she gives it. Her body moves without her thought, and she sings as she moves, and she thinks as she sings, and she moves as she writes.

And naked, she is more splendid in stillness than in motion. Her slight smile is still as a lake, waiting for some brave night creature to break the surface. Her compact body provides the necessities for her pleasure, and she nurtures her necessities as she waters your needs. You share what you know. You give each other pleasure and don't take it back. You feel the glory in your hearts. Doubts and sorrows seem silly and remote. For a few brief moments, you know why you live.

What a gal. Who could not love this subject? We, the researchers, can find no fault with this woman. Even the downs with her would be up. The blues would be sweet blues, and the ups would be the standard by which pleasure would be measured. She is a woman and a half, brother, and a man would be a fool to pass her by.

And speaking of passing things by, don't miss an in-depth interview with your author, coming up next!

future perfect

A candid conversation with the sallow opinionator and author of *Perfect World*, about sex, fame, fashion, rock and roll, and popular culture.

If anybody can epitomize the dark spirit of the tail end of the eighties, Ian Shoales would certainly like a shot at it. As he is fond of saying, with the least infectious grin we have ever encountered, "Make me an offer." Well, it looks like the world finally has. Just a short time ago, he was broke and asleep in a rich man's bed. Today, he could very well emerge as a sex symbol for women who don't demand too much of their fantasy lives. He has not recorded an album of over-produced love ballads, nor has he appeared on any magazine covers. Yet. This is amazing enough for a man of his pretensions. But all this may soon change.

Perfect World has outsold every book in the history of publishing. Ian Shoales' Perfect World of Wax is packing them in. It looks like Ian is becoming the very thing he dreads: a cultural phenomenon. Always on the lookout for ways to fill the white space between our covers, we sent Bob Cavett to track down Ian Shoales in San Francisco. Here's Bob's report.

After first convincing Ian I wasn't a creditor, I arranged to meet him at a little Nouveau place I'd been meaning to try. He was late, of course, so while I waited I had a flagon of Norsk Bleb, that tart Norwegian ale, and ordered for both of us: reddened blackfish, blackened redfish, and brackened brine balls. For a dinner wine I chose a Grosse Syrah, a very interesting wine. Mainly sediment, the wine is patted gently on the inner lip, between morsels of fish. This creates an uncontrollable pucker (duration twenty minutes) and a bright blue stain (which washes off easily), but the Syrah's unique body and texture make it an unforgettable sensation for today's palate.

When Ian arrived, midway through the Norsk Bleb,

he made no objection to anything I'd ordered, though he did pick rather sulkily (so it seemed to me) at his fish with the preheated fork, and muttered under his breath.

Finally we sat, he with his tankard of ale, I with my unblended coffee (one chews the bean, usually Turkish, while sipping lightly irradiated sparkling water) and marinated vodka; I switched on my Swiss microcassette machine and we began our conversation.

This tape was transcribed by a team of Mormon secretaries while I smoked my pipe and watched a semi-remarkable five hour videotape documentary on the composer Morton Subotnick.

NEW JERK

In your book, *Perfect World*, you choose Los Angeles as your setting.

SHOALES

Uh huh.

NEW JERK

Why L.A?

SHOALES

'Cause that's where I was.

NEW JERK

Could it be that you consider L.A. a metaphor for everything that is the best, and worst, about America?

SHOALES

Sure. That sounds about right. Who's paying for this?

NEW JERK

New Jerk.

SHOALES

I'll have another.

NEW JERK

Perfect World is unusual among action novels in that you, the protagonist, seem to be asleep throughout most of it.

SHOALES

I was tired. Being broke always makes me tired. When the going gets tough, the tough get sleepy.

NEW JERK

But things have certainly picked up.

SHOALES

Yeah. But I'm the kind of guy who can never believe good luck. Sometimes I think I'm still dreaming. That alarm is still going off, and the money I need is just slipping away.

NEW JERK

Uh huh. What's a Perfect evening for Ian Shoales?

SHOALES

I can't really describe a Perfect evening, Bob. I can only describe an imperfect evening.

NEW JERK

Which is?

SHOALES

This situation here pretty much fits the bill.

NEW JERK

There's a thought we could amortize over several sessions.

SHOALES

Sure, sure, sure.

NEW JERK

What about sex?

SHOALES

Well, not now, for God's sake, this is a restaurant, we're doing an interview.

NEW JERK

I wasn't suggesting you have sex with me.

SHOALES

Well, I certainly wasn't.

NEW JERK

Do you have trouble with women?

SHOALES

Who told you that? Diane? Just because I sold her Barbra Streisand albums to buy tickets to the Robert Cray concert? She should have been grateful. Why does every memory have to be a show tune? Does everything in life have to be a movie? Can't something be real, here, now, like love? Like passion? Like these tickets to the Robert Cray concert?

NEW JERK

Keep your voice down. People are watching.

SHOALES

I'd even settle for some real memories. We remember records, we remember movies. Where's the memory of the play of light and shadow on a moving naked back? Hey, that's not bad. What the hell am I drinking? Can I have another one?

WAITER

Ov karse.

SHOALES

What kind of accent is that anyway?

NEW JERK

What got you into criticism?

SHOALES

Nobody would take me seriously as a musician. I've also discovered that I'm incapable of holding a job.

NEW JERK

Fascinating! Why is that, do you think?

SHOALES

A combination of factors. Negative attitude, lack of attention span. I've found that spite and hatred give me a focus in life that I would otherwise lack.

NEW JERK

That's fantastic! You were a musician. Do you still play?

SHOALES

Yeah. I play acoustic guitar, but not in public. You need a certain sense of irony in the eighties even to pick up an acoustic guitar.

NEW JERK

Irony must be very important to you.

SHOALES

It must be. I've written a song about irony. Perhaps you'd care to hear it?

NEW JERK

Not really. But I'd like to peg your feelings re the CD/DAT controversy—

SHOALES

(SCREAMING) Anybody got a guitar in this dump?

SHUFFLING, BREAKING OF FURNITURE. IAN SHOALES OBTAINS A GUITAR FROM A STREET MUSICIAN IN THE DOORWAY, AND FORCES HIS WAY BACK INTO THE RESTAURANT. HE BEGINS TO SING, IN A PAINFUL WARBLING TENOR, REMINISCENT OF STING AFTER A BAD NIGHT, OR TOM WAITS AFTER A GOOD ONE. THE CHORDS MR. SHOALES USES TO ACCOMPANY HIMSELF HAVE NO APPARENT CONNECTION TO THE MELODY HE IS SINGING.

> *I'm just another white guy with nothing left to lose.*
> *A consumer with an attitude, too blasé for the blues.*
> *If my life was haunted I could justify my fears,*
> *But the force that hones a ghostly bone has never*
> *   entered here.*
> *All I got is food for thought: that's strictly a*
> *   take-out meal.*
> *I wish my life was haunted by the ghost of*
> *   something real.*

NEW JERK

Interesting. You've made your subtext explicit—

SHOALES

I'm not finished yet, pal.

SINGS

> *Irony! The final disguise of love!*
> *Its passion is a fashion we can slip on like a glove!*[2]

Everybody!

NEW JERK

Ha ha, Ian, nobody knows the words.

SHOALES

All right, we'll leave it to the imagination. Imagination is all we have, even if we only imagine the worst.

COMMOTION.

NEW JERK

Oh my God. It's the police!

SHOALES

An element of danger! I love danger if it doesn't hurt me. Wouldn't it be great if you could just walk through disasters. Oh you'd get a limp maybe, a scar or something sexy, like a map of where you've been. Nothing embarrassing like emotional scars, just a little salt, a little wound, enough to make you a romantic figure. That would be Perfect. Wouldn't that be just Perfect?

COP

Okay bud, get out from under the table. Grab your hat. We're going downtown.

[2]© 1988 Five Grown Men Music

Thank you, Ian.

SHOALES

Oh Ruth. Ruth, where are you?

suggested critical response

Because we will be in a Perfect World for most of this book, I'd like to be a grudging Samaritan to my colleagues out there. I know that critics not only have to wade through this thing, they have to have an opinion about it as well. Talk about your double-edged sword! So, to make that sword a little sharper, here is a glossary of useful critical terms.

Handy Adjectives: Transcendent, hypnotic, overwhelming, riveting, brilliant, bittersweet, flamboyant, surreal, rollicking, lavish, redemptive, wry, pointed, elegant, amusing, sharp, funny, sly, sexy, savvy, smart, steamy, jubilant, uplifting, Shoalesian, sophisticated, pointed, long.

Handy Nouns and Phrases: Searing indictment, real page-turner, couldn't put it down, edge-of-the-seat gut-churner, a blockbuster as timely as tomorrow's headlines, a good fast read, a helluva good read, a helluva good fast read, one helluva book, a helluva blockbuster, a helluva blockbuster as fast and timely as tomorrow's headlines, tells all, multicolored patchwork quilt of a novel.

Handy All-Purpose Verbs: Portray, reveal, bespeak, depict.

Handy Adjectives for Mixed Review (Optional): Annoying, trivial, uneven, flawed, flimsy, dogmatic, awful, false, malignant, forced, infuriating, disappointing, slight, Shoalesian.

Handy Left-Handed Compliments: For what this is, it's very good. A minor classic. A small jewel of a book. Challenging. Daunting. Not without redeeming features. For those of you who like their prose dense, this is the book to tackle. A small gem of a book. A polished diamond of a book. Tries vainly to live up to its brilliant premise. Effective.

Handy All-Purpose Review: Perfect World is that rare thing, a _____. *Perfect World* is as _____ as, well, _____. *Perfect World* deals frankly with _____ and the implications of _____. Finally someone has the courage to _____ openly about _____, with great _____ and unflagging _____. Not a false step mars this _____. Recommended.

perfect morning

"Ian? Ian?"

I turned at the sound of the voice.

"It's me, Ian—Ernie Doyle, your post-modernist." He was wheezing like a cold engine. "Slow down, will ya, I'm not in shape."

"What's up?" I asked. "I gotta get to the bank."

"This staple gun thing," he said. "What is it? A symbol or something? Swords into plowshares? Something like that?"

"I just thought it would come in handy. I never throw anything away."

"Symbolism is outmoded, Ian. You're treading on pretty thin ice here. What have you got? You got surrealism. You got expressionism. Your sense of experimentation is kind of dated, Ian. I thought you were supposed to be hip."

"I'll tell you something, Ernie. Ever since the time I was laid up sick with nothing to read but the *Carson of Venus* series by Edgar Rice Burroughs—well, let's just say it left a stain on the ice-cream suit of my aesthetics. The dry cleaners can't remove that stain, if you get my meaning, but I gotta wear *something* in public."

"I think you should lose the staple gun."

"Hold on," I said. "Let's bring in the writer."

Kapler appeared, or Kreisler. He had even darker circles under his eyes than I did. He was carrying a carton of white-out. He was groaning.

" 'Can we lose the staple gun without disturbing narrative flow?' I said. 'What narrative flow?' he said," he said.

"Cut that out," I said. "It makes me nervous. Lose the staple gun, get a word processor, and get out of my way. I gotta get to the bank by ten or they're gonna stop payment."

I rechecked the checks as I walked away. They were BunniBank checks. BunniBank had originally been PetroChemiUniBank, but they'd merged with BunniBurgers, a slow chain of fast foods, and purchased by ProCorGenTel. With branches on every block, they were certainly convenient, but they only had drive-through service. I had no car. I walked over to the BunniBank between Sunset and Hollywood on La Brea. The red LED display above the teller's booth told me it was nine: fifty-four. I wandered over to the teller's booth and pressed my nose against the glass. SMILE! YOU'RE ON VIDEOTAPE! read a sign, its heartiness not quite concealing its aggressive paranoia. On the video monitor below the sign, I could see me, pressing my face against the glass, watching myself on television. Not *my* idea of good video.

On a whim, I removed Destiny Commander from my pocket, pointed it at the video monitor and pressed a button. To my surprise, the monitor began switching channels every five seconds, and Destiny Commander began to speak to me.

"Good morning, Mr. Shoales. What you are seeing on the monitor is just the tip of the iceberg of my capabilities. Let me slide back the panel to display my full range."

"Better snap it up," I said. "The bank's gonna open any minute."

"System One. Home entertainment. One-touch convenience for your every audio/visual need. System Two. Hands-free tele-communications! System Three. Memory Jogging and Three-Dimensional Visualizations of possible futures! System Four—"

It droned on. This thing was typical of our new technology. It allows us to spend more time thinking about how many channels we have than about what appears on those channels. We shop for cut-rate long-distance services, and still have nothing to say. We brag about the ease of our word-processing program, but sit blank in front of the green screen, waiting for ideas to travel magically through the circuits.

"—System Seven. With required top secret code, you can turn powerful weapons on and off with a mere vocal command. See your local Federal agent for details—"

This caught my ear.

"Wait a minute," I said. "What are you anyway?"

"Things are never what they seem," said Destiny Commander. "But now you can put reality's disguises to work for you. With Destiny Commander! The last word in lei—"

A teller was approaching the window. I clicked off the device.

"Yes, sir?" she said.

I stepped up to the ATM, a bright fiberglass sculpture shaped like a cartoon rabbit's head.

"Can I help you, sir?" The woman's voice seemed to come from the rabbit's mouth.

"I want to cash a check," I said.

"Do you have an account with us, sir?"

"No. But it's a BunniBank check."

"Would you like to open an account? You get a FunnyBunny."

"What's a funny bunny?" I asked.

A gray furry arm emerged from the ATM and waved at me. I heard the whir of machinery almost disguised by loud tinny music. The bunny ears wiggled. "Hiya partner," said a prerecorded high-pitched voice. "Ask us about our Ginny Maes!"

"I just want to cash a check," I said.

"It's me again," came the cashier's voice. "You get a lottery ticket with every five thousand deposited, and your choice of FunnyBunny or high-powered rifle!"

"Just the check," I said, slipping one in to her.

"My my," she said metallically. "Look at all those zeroes."

"Wait," I said, slipping in the other check.

"Nine billion dollars?" she asked. "That's a lot of money. Do you have a current driver's license and major credit card?"

"My license has expired," I said, "but I haven't. Ha ha ha ha!

I've also got a membership card for Radio Shack's Battery Club."

"Well," she sighed, "I guess we have to cash it. Would you like this in BunnyMoney, redeemable at most major department stores? They qualify you for discounts."

"Real money, please, and a BunniBurger with cheese, while I'm waiting, and a chocolate shake."

"Would you like fries with that?"

"If I'd wanted fries, I would have asked for them," I said, annoyed.

"Thank you sir. Please hold."

Loud stupid music came out of the rabbit's mouth. A steaming cheeseburger emerged on the rabbit's tongue, with a tepid milk shake.

I suddenly lost my appetite. I threw the lunch package on the ground, and examined Destiny Commander thoughtfully.

"You should really wipe the grease off your hands if you're going to handle me," it warned. "I'm a delicate piece of equipment."

"Listen, pal," I said. "You'd better be built to take punishment if you're going to capture today's youth market."

"I'm only a prototype," it apologized.

"Sir?" came the woman's voice.

I tucked Destiny Commander in my sock (*the* safest place from pickpockets, that's a tip) and turned back to the ATM. I really don't know which made me feel sillier, talking to a big plastic bunny, or to a palm-sized gaggle of microchips that sounded vaguely like Burgess Meredith. It was a toss-up, really.

"Sir?" said the woman's voice. "We don't have enough cash on hand to cover this. We're sending around to the other branches for more. Now, you're sure you are who you say you are? This isn't a forgery or an attempt to steal from us?"

"No."

"I *guess* you're honest," she said. "You have an honest face. It's not a very *pleasant* face, but it's *honest*."

A car drove up and parked in the take-out lane. A portly guy got out of the back seat. He looked a little bit like Mr. Dithers. Taller.

"Your name Shoales?" he barked.

"Who's asking?" I said.

"Well, me," he said. "I am. We've got a problem. I'm the bank manager."

"There a problem with the check?"

"No, the check is fine, the problem is the cash. How do you want it?"

I hadn't given it much thought. I said, "I thought maybe you could put a million dollars in a briefcase if you used twenties, hundreds, and thousands."

"There's the problem, Mr. Shoales," he said. "We'd need nine thousand briefcases."

"I see," I said. "And I don't even have one briefcase."

"You could buy one."

"I don't have any money," I said. "Yet."

"Well," he said. "Let me see. If we make it all thousands, we could probably fit three million per briefcase. That would bring us down from nine to three thousand briefcases."

"That's a help," I said.

"Why don't I have my secretary call around? I'm sure we can have some briefcases delivered. Now. How are you going to carry around that much cash?"

"Boy," I said. "I really haven't thought this out, have I? Wait. How many briefcases can fit in a limo?"

"By golly," he chuckled, "I haven't tried that since my college days. Back then, it was two hundred. But that was cramming, and the briefcases weren't filled with thousand-dollar bills."

"What were they crammed with?"

"Goldfish."

"Well, let's say fifty briefcases per limo. I mean, we gotta leave room for the driver and a passenger."

"That means we need, let's see, three thousand briefcases, fifty per limo—sixty limos, with drivers. This will take a half-hour to set up."

"Maybe I'll get something *good* to eat," I said. "Can you loan me a thousand? I'll go over to New Food and buy some yogurt."

"Sure," said Mr. Dithers. "No problem."

He snapped his fingers and the ATM spat a thousand-dollar bill into my hand. I started to walk away.

"When they get here," I shouted back, "make sure the drivers lock up. And give them each a thousand for their trouble. The coffee's on me."

perfect day
_____ New Food is a new concept in convenience stores. Instead of actual food, the aisles display photographs of food, each with an identifying code number; the actual food is stored in a vast underground freezer/microwave chamber. I could see myself, on the bank of monitors in the rear of the store, writing down numbers in the special pad. A calm deep voice spoke from hidden loudspeakers: "Color photographs of you and your family shopping are provided free of charge with every purchase over twenty dollars. Smile! And thank you for shopping New Food."

I totted up my choices in the Express Lane: one Tall Boy Lemon-Grass Thai Ale (#0012) and one Blueberry Yorgi Yogurt Stir 'N Slurp (#7617). Tiny robot fingers dragged my numbers through a red adding light.

"Has New Food filled your needs?" asked a bored teenage voice.

"Where's that voice coming from?" I asked the impatient housewife behind me.

"Just say yes," she said. "If you say no, the computer gets confused."

"Yes," I said.

"That'll be a buck fifty-nine," said the voice. A brushed aluminum tray elevated with a hum from the surface of the conveyor belt. I placed the thousand-dollar bill in the tray; the tray descended and disappeared.

"Nothing smaller?" came the voice.

"Sorry."

"Well, I can't change this. Some jerk in the bank across the street just cashed a big check, and every dollar in the city is going into his pocket."

"It's the smallest I've got," I said.

Suddenly his voice was amplified throughout the store.

"Checker," it said. "Eviction and Restorage, Express Lane."

"Now you've done it," said the housewife. "He's called the Food Police."

"Wait a minute," I said. "I'm hungry. I'll swap you for the suit."

"That's against New Food policy," hissed the housewife.

"That suit is def," said the voice. "It's so nerdy it's hip. Put it in."

I stepped out of my pants, avoiding the eyes of the housewife, and slipped off my jacket. I still had my shoes (two sturdy Street-huggers,™ built for walking) my Jockeys, and my Yves St. Laurent powder-blue cotton shirt, which I'd borrowed from a former room-mate three years before, and the green tie (of course), a gift. I stuffed the clothes into the tray, took my purchases and thousand-dollar bill, and walked out of the machine-driven chill of New Food into the heat of the larger machine—L.A.

I was starting to sweat. I took off my shirt and sat down on a traffic bump. I cracked a cold one, sucked yogurt. I thought about L.A.—the girls and cars all stunned by heat, submerged in envy, beaten. Ambition here is thwarted and fed by sleep, smog, and sun. I love it. I love the idea of it. You sit poolside while the bucks roll in. You catch the gravy train and let the good times roll.

But there, in that parking lot, where heat made the illusion of ripples on the black asphalt, the poolside vision seemed the most foolish of dreams. And even if you could make that vision real, you'd have to spend the rest of your life in a car, reliving poolside memories, trapped in a fender-to-fender crawl. A poolside memory is a poor reward for a life spent in pursuit of poolside memories.

The cars out here are a nomad's dream: slick, optioned to the max. But the climate is for old people and reptiles. The rest of us must drive—drive and dream of some cool place beyond those scorched and hazy mountains, some stupid end-of-the-movie paradise—*Brazil*'s Brazil, or that psychedelic glade at the end of *Blade Runner*. We steer our machines toward a Baptist's idea of heaven. We believe we can get there without wings. That's the promise. All you need is four-wheel drive and an Eddie Bauer catalog. You work for the end of working, you work for the hope you'll never have to work again.

I stood up. Across from me was a blasted fenced-in zone where some building had been. In front of that fence, a pudgy drunk white woman in a platinum wig was screaming at a very thin black man. Her voice drifted my way like a bird's hungry scream on the wind. She threw her purse at the black man and marched down the street. The black man hung back, muttering to himself. He took a few steps in the opposite direction, then wheeled around, picked up her purse, and slouched after her. She sensed or knew he was following her, turned, and screamed at him some more. He kept coming anyway, mumbling and looking around to make sure nobody was watching. It was a motion-filled Polaroid of potential abuse. It was a scenario for murder.

"How about it, Destiny Commander," I said. "Can you switch this channel?"

"Move it!" a bullhorn barked. Two cops sat in a car in the far end of the parking lot. I glanced up. "Yeah, you. Keep it moving." I kept it moving, and started walking back to the bank. The most a cop hopes for is: *Please don't let it happen on my beat. Get that leather flapping, bud. It's on wheels, sister. Die somewhere else.* I tucked my thousand-dollar bill next to Destiny Commander and crossed the street.

A long line of gleaming limos awaited me. The chauffeurs stood beside them, hands clasped behind their backs, watching me. Mr. Dithers approached me.

"I think we have it all packed, Mr. Shoales," he said, "right down to the last penny. You like the briefcases? They're Vuitton."

"Vuitton?" I said. "What's wrong with good old Samsonite? You think I'm made of money?"

"Pretty much," he admitted.

I turned my back on him and asked the driver nearest me, "What's your name?"

"Sarge," he said.

"Is every limo driver named Sarge?" I asked.

"Sarge or Doc," he said. "You're Mr. Shoales?"

I nodded.

"We'll need some proof before you can take possession of all this," he said.

I reached for my wallet, then remembered I was wearing nothing but my underwear, socks, and shoes. "I left my wallet back at the store," I said.

Sarge frowned. "Okay, boys! Back to the yard!"

"Wait!" I said. "You know the Ian Shoales commentaries?"

"Of course," he said. "Every man, woman, and child in America has committed at least one of them to memory."

"If I were to give you a commentary, would that be sufficient ID?"

"Yes," he said slowly. "But I warn you, the Shoales style is inimitable. If you're an impostor, you will be found out, and turned over to the proper authorities."

"I wish I had a TelePrompTer," I said. I swallowed, stood back, and recited:

---

op/ed from ian

"The Summer Lineup"

Twentieth Century Shoales, a wholly owned subsidiary of ShoalesCo, an offshore corporation with a mailing address in the Cayman Islands, is proud to present its summer movie lineup. All we need is an investor or two and these movies will be out of the theaters and on the cassette racks before you can say "Phantom income." If you're an investor who wants out of the oil business and into a lower tax bracket, hey, we've got a limited partnership deal for you. We're ready to produce, well, not blockbusters, really, these movies won't bust the block, but they just might stroll down to the corner and be back in time to show up on cable. Checkbooks ready? Here they are.

Bob Schwarzenegger, Arnold's little brother, is *The Litigator*. Hire him for a lawyer or he'll break your arms. His out-of-court settlement is a MAC-10. He's the warrior-lawyer who—all right, I can see you're putting your pen away, nice pen too, is that a Cross? How about this one? Bob Cruise, Tom's little brother, in *Bottom Gun,* the true story of today's fightin' navy! See Bob swab the decks! See Bob get pasty and overweight on a starchy military diet! How about this? A film by Bob Hughes, John's little brother, *A Long Day Off's Journey to a Pink Breakfast,* with Nelson Judd, Elmo St. Fire, Bobbi Ringwald, Bobbi Sheedy, and Harry Dean Stanton as Keenan Wynn. No? How about Bobby Bob DeNiro in *The Vanessa Redgrave Story,* with Bob Hoffman as young Vanessa and Bobbi Redgrave as Dustin Hoffman? Or Bob Stallone in *Everybody's Psycho!* featuring Richard Crenna as the guy who says, "How come *I* don't get a little bitty machine gun?"

You like foreign movies? Me neither, but we got Roberto Fellini's *Large Dead Fish Washed Up on Shore,* and Bob Blier's *The Wacky Nihilist,* with balloons, wheat fields, wistful accordion music, breasts, and middle-aged men shrugging their shoulders because Miou Miou won't go to bed with them.

How about Bob Murray, Bobbi Streep, Bob Alda, even Joe Bob Bond, the hillbilly spy, in *Voyages of the Starship Bob?* We got guaranteed rave reviews from Bob Shoales and Bob Joe Briggs. All this and more from Big Bob Pictures. Remember. If there's a Bob in the picture, it's a Big Bob Picture. I love you, you're beautiful, let's have lunch. I gotta go.

---

our tale resumes

As I caught my breath, I saw that all the chauffeurs had taken off their caps, in reverence.

"Forgive us for doubting you, Mr. Shoales," said Sarge. "Get in the back, and let's ride!" His eyes shone with excitement.

"No," I said. "I'd rather walk for awhile. Have the caravan follow me. I want to go down the boulevard and think."

He saluted me. I returned the salute, and spun around in an about-face, which, while well-executed, only spun me halfway around. This brought me face to face with the remains of BunniBank. Burly workmen were already at work, bringing down the flimsy structure. A sledgehammer smashed the face of the FunnyBunny ATM. It squealed in a humorous imitation of pain.

Mr. Dithers and a well-dressed woman stood beside me to watch it come down.

"This is the end of BunniBank?" I asked.

"*You* did it, Mr. Shoales," he said. "You put a pretty big dent in our assets. We were ripe for a takeover. For some reason there's a lot of raiders out there who just love to accumulate other people's debts."

"What's going up instead," I wondered.

"A dry cleaners and one-stop photo center," said the woman.

I looked at her.

"I'm your teller," she said. "Cindy."

"Hey, I'm sorry if I cost you your jobs," I said.

"Don't worry about it," said Mr. Dithers. "I tipped some brokers about the takeover and my commission should keep me in Italian suits for the rest of my life."

"And I've been embezzling for years," said Cindy. "I had to, on what they were paying me."

"Doesn't anybody earn an honest buck anymore?" I asked.

"Probably not," admitted the bank manager. "What are you going to do with your money, anyway?"

I thought about that, as I watched the rubble of the bank go up in flames. The workmen were erecting a chain-link fence around a tower of fire.

"I could help defray the national debt," I said.

The manager snorted. "The national debt is well over a trillion dollars now, Ian," he said.

"It doesn't mean anything," said the teller soothingly in my ear. "It's just numbers on a piece of paper."

"You could give away the entire nine billion dollars to the feds," said the manager, "and it would only cover one-fifth of the interest, and that gets bigger every day."

"Plus you'd still have to pay taxes on it," said the teller.

"Let's consider the national debt as one of those stretch limos," said the manager. "Your money would pay for maybe a spare tire."

"Not even," said the teller. "A jack maybe. No. A cassette for the tape deck. No—"

"It's been great talking to you," I said. "I gotta go."

The L.A. sun, invisible in the vastness of brown smog, seemed to be feeding its heat to these flames. My ale was getting warm. I was getting sleepy again. I started to walk, nearly naked, into the growing heat of the full day.

PART THREE

Noon

in which we attempt to spend our money and
our time

*F*ood *for* *T*hought

Some say, "The glass of water is half-empty." Some say, "It's half-full." I say, "A glass with some water in it. So what?"

—Selmer Lesker

Which will you be when the money's gone?
Who will you be when the money's all gone?
Convict or cowboy?

—Willy Dalton, "Convicts and Cowboys"

perfect pitch

Commercial; 60 seconds
(NEW FOOD)

ANNOUNCER:

Ian will be right back with more fun and information, right after this important word from our sponsor.

VIDEO	AUDIO
A YOUNG, WELL-DRESSED PROFESSIONAL SPOKESMODEL WHEELS HER EMPTY GROCERY CART THROUGH THE AISLES OF NEW FOOD. SHE NOTICES THE CAMERA AND SPEAKS.	SPOKESMODEL Hi! I'm not a real person, but I play one on television. I pretend to go shopping so you can pretend *you're* on television when *you* go shopping. Well, you don't have to pretend anymore. At New Food, you're on television too!
SHE WHEELS HER EMPTY CART OUT OF FRAME.	

CUT TO:

TYPICAL HOUSEWIFE IN FRONT OF NEW FOOD, HOLDING A LARGE BAG OF GROCERIES. SUPER: "MRS. LUCILLE JOHNSON, ANAHEIM"	LUCILLE JOHNSON I was standing there comparing tuna prices and the next thing I knew I was in a New Food commercial saying, "I was in a New Food commercial." This is no joke!

CUT TO:

SPOKESMODEL IN STORE, NOW
DRESSED IN AEROBICS OUTFIT.
AS SHE SPEAKS, SHE PUSHES
HER CART OUT OF FRAME.

SPOKESMODEL
Who's watching you at New
Food? Maybe your next-door
neighbor, maybe our security
staff, maybe even a Hollywood producer!

CUT TO:

CLOSE-UP OF GENERIC CANS
OF DIET SODA.

ANNOUNCER (VOICE-OVER)
This week's TV bargain: generic light, two for ninety-
nine!

CUT TO:

CLOSE-UP OF SPOKESMODEL

SPOKESMODEL
When you know you're
being watched you know
you'll watch your weight!

CUT TO:

CLOSE-UP OF GENERIC ASPIRIN
BOTTLES.

ANNOUNCER (VOICE-OVER)
And ibuprofen substitutes
half off when you say—

CUT TO:

CLOSE-UP OF SPOKESMODEL.
CAMERA PULLS BACK. SHE
JUMPS IN THE AIR.

SPOKESMODEL
I saw it on television!

FREEZE-FRAME OF
SPOKESMODEL

IN MIDAIR, "NEW FOOD" LOGO
BEHIND HER.

ANNOUNCER (VOICE-OVER)
—Aren't you a New You?
Don't you need New Food?

ANNOUNCER (TAG):

And now, we return to *Perfect World.*

the city of angels

Funny. Just a couple years ago, back in San Francisco, I was walking briskly down the street trying to think of ways to make money. I'd made a lot of mistakes in my time and it seemed like television made a lot of money from mistakes, by airing them as Blooper shows. What I needed, I thought, was a way to turn my lifestyle bloopers into Major Bloopers; I needed what network execs call a "high concept," which is a sentence that looks good in *T.V. Guide*, like "Poor Black Kid Moves in with Rich White People and Then the Fun Begins," or "Stupid Woman Moves in with Two Lecherous Men and Then the Fun Begins," or even "Wacky Teen Moves in with Chimp and Then the Fun Begins." And then— a million-dollar idea struck me.

What if you had a Blooper show in which everybody did everything *right?* If you do a Blooper correctly, isn't that a Blooper in its own right? An Anti-Blooper? A kind of Zen Blooper?

In my mind's eye I was pitching Zen Bloopers to a network producer, trying to explain to him just when, exactly, the Fun Begins, when—right there on the street—a very attractive woman in a trenchcoat stepped in front of me, shoved a microphone in my face, and asked, "What would you like to see more of on 'Foul-ups, Bleeps, and Blunders'?"

I just couldn't believe it. There I'd been thinking about Bloopers, and a Blooper person stopped me right there on the street! I spotted the video camera a split second later, and I was about to pitch my Zen Blooper concept to the Blooper people, when the Blooper lady slipped off her trenchcoat with a frozen smile, and stood before me in a skimpy bikini. I could see the goosebumps rise on her flat stomach. She said, "What would you like to see more of on 'Foul-ups, Bleeps, and Blunders'?" Her smile was slipping. She was clenching her teeth to keep them from chattering. I said, "Lady, you're not getting paid enough." I turned to the camera and said, "Are you people heartless animals? You've made this poor woman stand in her underwear on a freezing San Francisco street, just on the off-chance some stupid libidinous male might gawk at her, so you could get a good shot of the poor sap's double take." As I gathered breath to say more, someone said, "Cut," the woman said, "Can I put my coat back on?" and the whole crew vanished down an alley. I continued on my way.

I watched all the Blooper shows for months, but my face never showed up, which proved to me that a non-Blooper on a Blooper show is *in fact* a Blooper, but a true Blooper doesn't qualify as a Blooper. My sad conclusion was: *Zen Bloopers will not make me any money.* Not making money is, of course, Zen Capitalism, the same way as having money and not spending it is Blooper Capitalism. That pretty much seemed to describe the situation that steamy L.A. noon.

My theory of capitalism has always been: *Every buck you make is a buck somebody else isn't making.* This obviously false economic theory has allowed me to talk myself out of a lot of jobs. And now that I actually *had* money, what could I do with it? I know you're supposed to put your money to work for you, but an amount that large seemed to have worked enough. It seemed kind of tuckered, frankly. Over the purr of the limos behind me, I could almost hear the soft crinkle of exhausted money. Nine billion dollars (give or take a couple hundred thousand for expenses) were creaking and moaning like the masts of a pirate ship. Lordy.

There were so many ways to use the cash: bribery, accumulation of possessions, the repayment of loans. The repayment of loans? Eighty-six that idea, Jacks and Jills. What would that do to my reputation? I'm a hand-to-mouth kind of guy, not to mention untrustworthy.

So there I was, stumbling down the street, half-naked, scorched by the heat of the invisible sun, blasted by the fires of burning BunniBanks, thinking, *Maybe I'm too old to change my spots, to learn new tricks. Should I just give it all away? To whom? Who wants it?*

A bright light blinded me. A microphone was thrust into my face.

"Ian Shoales," came a woman's voice, smooth and fast. "How does it feel to have nine billion dollars?"

"What do my feelings matter?" I asked. "Are my emotions news?"

A man's voice came from my left: "Mr. Shoales, I'm with the Internal Revenue Service. If you'll just give us two-thirds of your limos, we'll call it even."

I started to walk faster. Three more cameras appeared, and a thicket of microphones, like steel mushrooms.

"Mr. Shoales! Mr. Shoales!"

I started to run.

I'd been so lost in thought I hadn't noticed that a crowd had gathered. There was a born-again panting on my left, trying to keep up. He was holding a Bible in his big strong hands and gasping, "Send it in, send it in! Every dollar comes back twice, guaranteed by Jesus!" On my right, a gray-faced man in a leisure suit staggered as he ran. "My insurance lapsed," he shouted, "and I need a bypass. Can you help me out?"

Behind me I could see a politician's wife hitching up her elegant gown as she trotted after me. "I'm heading a drive—" she shouted, then tripped over a junkie, nodding and sagged on the curb. "Just say no!" she told him as she fell headlong.

"No!" said the junkie. "I need twenty-nine cents!"

A gangly kid with acne had hold of my leg and wouldn't let go. "Five bucks, man, that's all. I need it for a date." As I pried his fingers off, I saw a weeping farmer, cracked hands outstretched, who said, "It hurts my pride."

A phalanx of cashiers moved in on my left. A platoon of landlords waved leases. I thought I saw every girlfriend I'd ever had, in the shimmering haze of the middle distance, marching toward me down the middle of the street. There were lawyers in three-piece suits; agents in their sockless Guccis; and parking meters, expired. They all wanted a piece of what I had.

I kicked away the gangly kid and jumped over a beggar. "Feed me," he cried weakly as I stumbled away. I dodged around a mother with three kids, as she screamed, "I have no place to stay, and if I go back he'll kill me!"

A pale man in turquoise had me by the waist. "Twenty acres, Mr. Shoales, prime land in Texas!" From a window above, an old woman was showing me her purse, turned inside out and upside down. Dust and bugs were falling from its depths. "They took every penny, mister, they took my last dime!"

A gypsy with almond eyes showed me a handkerchief. "Give me half and I'll make it all clean."

I wriggled away and sprinted. Behind me I heard scattered shouts:

"I lost on the game show!"

"I bet every dime!"

"I can prove who killed Kennedy. The proof is for sale!"

"Guns to kill Castro!"

"Help me! I missed the boat!"

I turned down a side street. My way was blocked by two limousines, not mine. Tan men with moussed hair emerged from each limo, each holding a MAC-10. I stopped in my tracks.

"We have good times for sale," said the man on the left, setting his weapon on automatic. "But with no cash there's no customers. We don't take checks, you know."

The man on the right said, "That is my cash, man, I've had runners depositing that stuff for months. It's gotta go to Panama and Switzerland and the Cayman Islands, man. How's it gonna move if you're sitting on it?"

"That's *my* money, man," said the man on the left.

"Mine," said the other. They turned on each other and started firing. I ducked into an alley and kept running. I stopped to catch my breath. My lungs were on fire.

I looked up. Above me in the sky, pushing through the haze of brown, like wasps wriggling backwards from their hives, tiny white shapes wiggled down. And in the middle of each shape was a tinier squirming dot, like a black ant feasting on a marshmallow, or a pinpoint of pupil in a disembodied eye. I'd already used more metaphors than most people use in a lifetime and I still didn't know what they were. They descended further. I suddenly heard the chop of helicopters and the screaming roar of engines in the sky. They were parachutes. And those black shapes were men. Yes, I could make them out. They were holding something that glinted in reflected light. Guns. What were these men? They weren't honest citizens, that's for sure. These figures were anonymous; honest citizens are never anonymous.

One of them landed at my feet. He was dressed in black from head to foot, and his weapon dripped grease that fell in transparent blobs on the asphalt. "Money for the struggle," he said. Another landed behind me. "Guns!" he said. "Bombs!" They were terrorists. I wasn't afraid—yet. Terrorists only kill what they cannot have. They're identity vampires, who consume the lives of others, and cash is the coffin that keeps them alive. I backed away, smiling and nodding.

My question had been answered, all right. Who needs my money? Everybody. Except the media, of course. All they needed was a good segment to feed the hungry teevee mouth. Money provides that too. Every fool wants money. And I'm the king of every fool in need. I'm the biggest link in this chain of fools: a fool and his money.

"Hey fool," came another voice.

I looked around. Five black kids stood ahead of the pack, all wearing black t-shirts faded brown from the sun, and threadbare hightop sneakers. None of them had skateboards, thank God, I *hate* skateboards, but the oldest kid, he couldn't have been more than ten, had a gun.

Behind them the pack closed in. At their head I could see Burst and Sunder. They each raised gray machine guns and they smiled as they advanced. The politician's wife held her high heels in her hand. She came to a halt and pointed at the black kid in front of me.

"Oh my God!" she screamed. "Negroes! Watch out!"

The kid had a tiny shiny pistol, and he pointed it at my head.

"Give me all your money, fool," he said.

your top ten countdown

———————————— *top ten phrases I would never hear in a perfect world*

1. Surprise, Ian, remember me? And this is your son! Say "Hi Daddy," sweetie!

2. You have an interesting aura.

3. You're under arrest.

4. Have you found the investment plan that's right for you?

5. Wake up.

6. If you don't love yourself, how can you love anyone else?

7. I'm sorry to call this late, but I had to talk to you.

8. Give me your money.

9. Do you believe in love at first sight?

10. Welcome to Vietnam, gentlemen. The bunkers are on your left. Start running.

perfect criminals

——————————— I looked up. The hole at the end of the pistol was a tunnel with no light. Beyond this small boy with a gun, the big boys with big guns, Burst and Sunder, tiptoed slowly closer. One of the braver cameramen was circling the circle of black children, trapping everything on tape. Beside him was a guy who looked like Mark Focus from *Putney Swope*; he had a Nikon with a strobe. He crouched like a lizard, his eyes slitted as he sized up his shots, his mouth slowly moving gum around. And beyond this circle, the crowd of money-seekers had stopped in their tracks, holding their breath, watching. I looked down at the black kid.

"You ought to be ashamed of yourself," I said. "You scared me half out of my wits."

"Huh," he said. "You sound like my mama."

"And what would your mother say," I said, putting my hands on my hips, "if she found you out here with a gun, sticking people up?"

He mumbled something.

"Speak up," I said.

"She wouldn't like it."

"Of course she wouldn't. We should never do anything our mother wouldn't like. That's a good moral rule of thumb."

One of the little boys behind him started to cry. "I don't have no mama," he said.

"You stop that, Roy," said the kid with the gun. "What's

wrong with you?" he said to me. "You're supposed to give me the money."

"Where'd you get that gun anyway?" I asked.

"Brother," he said.

"Does your brother know you have it?"

"Gonna bring it back," he said.

"We're sorry, mister," said the motherless child.

"We wasn't gonna hurt you," said the kid with a gun. "It ain't even loaded. See?" He pointed it in the air and it went off with a tiny pop. The kid screamed in terror, dropped the gun, and all the kids ran off. Burst and Sunder both dropped their weapons in panic, and the cameraman and photographer both dropped their cameras. They ran off crouching, like stringers in Beirut, into the mob of seekers, who milled into each other and stumbled away screaming, like a Tokyo mob in the wake of Godzilla.

I ducked behind a garbage can. The little silver gun jerked on its hair trigger in a little lazy circle, spitting bullets. The two machine guns stitched random patterns on the walls, smashing storefronts as they spun like spinning tops in the middle of the street. The camera's strobe flashed as it spun, a demon looking for souls to steal, and the video camera lay on its side, its indifferent eye unconnected to anything human, just recording, just laying down tape until everything spun slowly to a stop. Finally the only sound was the faint whirring of tape, and the metallic spin of one lonely shell casing, which whirled in tiny circles, like a fading echo of the blasting guns, a parody. Then there was silence and the smell of cordite. Distant sirens started up and moved closer. Someone tapped my shoulder. I turned. It was Sarge, the driver, looking grim.

"They're trying to break into the limos," he said. "Instructions?"

"Pull the wagons into a circle," I said. "And hold them off as long as you can."

Something split the air above my head, and I heard the crack of a gunshot a moment later. Out of the corner of my eye I saw Burst and Sunder once more, with new weapons, faster weapons, and I was up and running, through the glass doorway that was exploding all around me, past the poster on the ground, a picture of a happy penguin, shot through the heart: COME ON IN, IT'S KOOL

INSIDE! And through two double doors, which flapped shut behind me, and then I found myself in darkness, and alone.

spur of the moment

Before me was a woman twelve feet tall, wearing only an orange merry widow. She was kneeling on a green shag carpet and smiling. A giant man walked toward her, his head out of frame. "What's that I see?" said a highly insincere woman's voice, from fuzzy speakers above me. "Is that all for me?" A zipper unzipped. Variations ensued.

Just my luck. I'd wandered into a porno movie. Well, at least it was a movie. I settled into my seat and pulled my head down, out of the potential line of fire.

Pornography is the subtext of television commercials—a world that might open to you if you buy the bright boxes: the perfume, the beer, the wine, the clothing. It's a Perfect World of Sex, a world without speech (the only true word is "Yes!"), a world of availability. But it's a *faux* world as cheap as a TV diamond; it's a quick copy of desire, without a real thing in it. Pornography can't afford the finer things: good actors, sharp clothing, nice cars. And if hardcore *could* afford the perfect things, they would only be removed. Articles of clothing are only left on the body for effect: high heels, garter belts, pink teddies—clothes which accent a naked state. The body is the only subject here, the Perfect Body, a body divorced from any kind of social context, a body whose only function is to be rewarded.

The giant man spilled his seed on the giant woman's stomach. I saw her act like this was just about the biggest thrill she'd ever had. Once upon a time all the popcorn was buttered; now it's all as greasy as a machine gun, and every last pleasure in life is slowly degraded.

I remembered the first movie I ever saw: *The Searchers*. Little Natalie Wood, kidnapped and raised by Indians. John Wayne and Jeffrey Hunter have pursued her for years, through her childhood, past her puberty, into her savage adulthood. Will the Duke rescue her, or kill her? *She slept with the Indian chief,* thinks grim John Wayne, her movie uncle, a man consumed by racial hatred. *She slept with Scar.* Natalie Wood runs in terror, outlined against a glaring bank of desert, a blasted cruel landscape with no mercy in it. And there is John Wayne, yonder on his swift pony, riding her down. She cowers against the wall of the cave as John Wayne bears down on her. And Jeffrey Hunter is nowhere in sight!

I was eight years old. I thought that he would kill her. But he scooped her up like the strongest daddy in the world, and lifted her over his head until her head blocked the sun.

Thirty years and more have passed. And I watched the in-and-out porno close-ups of flesh—in the back seat, on the pool table, in the pool, on the rug, on the desk, on some padded shelf in hell. Any time. Any place. Any way. It doesn't matter. I've taken classes in "film," and I've seen *The Searchers* maybe once a year since I was eighteen. I see now the racism, the stupid buddy-buddy jokes John Ford liked so much, and all that clumsy stage Irish lamebrain humor, the sexism, and the clumsy storytelling, but I still feel every time that moment of relief that John Wayne is not going to kill that girl. I see the pain of that cowboy alienation. I see open doorways exposing the vast blasted beauty of the desert. I see the warrior, and the uncle, and a wall of names in Washington, D.C.

How do we divorce our memories from the movies? Why do we want to? Isn't this what we are? Glamour and Shopping and The Fall of Saigon? The liar at the hearing and the hero on the t-shirt—aren't they the same man? Art and Commerce and A Man Who Can't Walk Tall Under Another Man's Sky, and A Cowboy So Bitter No Sweetness Can Touch Him? Utter Sin and Deep Honor and Popcorn With Butter? What is America? Families on a merry-go-round spinning so fast the children fly off into the night. A wasp in the baby's room. A maiden on the tracks. Sweet dreams of escape. Bitter dreams of rescue. Perfect Stories.

On the screen in front of me a woman pretended to have an orgasm. If all I want to do is crawl back inside my eight-year-old body, to watch John Wayne turn his back on a happy ending that doesn't need him, to see him walk through the open door, away from us all, into the white sand and sun, if I want to forget for two brief hours the switches and twitches of the grown-ups we've become, to stumble blinking from the matinee into the harsh afternoon light, where is the harm? Where is the harm in that? I don't know, pals and gals. It's all rock and roll to me.

Something whined past my head. I found myself in the harsh glare of afternoon light, the movie theater behind me, a dumpster on my left. Bullets ripped through the steel exit door; I could feel the tiny breeze of their passage. I didn't think twice. I lifted the lid of the dumpster and climbed inside.

suggested critical response
Mr. Shoales has taken himself off the airwaves long enough to display a prose style that is a lean mean fighting machine. He juggles various points of view, all of them his, with elegance, grace, and wit. If he doesn't get a Pulitzer for this latest effort, there is no justice and it is indeed an imperfect world. Four stars. Satisfactory. Ten out of ten. Highly recommended. Very pleasurable. A great book. Probably the best book I have ever read.

in the dumps
My heart pounded in that steely darkness. I breathed through my mouth.

"Who am I?" I whispered to myself. "Franz Kafka or Eddie Haskell?"

"You're Ian Shoales, man," came a voice on my left. "Wake up."

"Destiny Commander?" I asked. In the excitement I'd forgotten all about it. I removed it from my sock. "Was that you?"

"Not me," said Destiny Commander. "I recommend changing your socks, by the way."

"Wow," said the voice on my left. "That thing sounds like the Penguin on 'Batman.' "

"Who are you?" I asked.

"Randee," he whispered back. "That's with two E's, like the river."

"Here," said Destiny Commander. "Let me illuminate this person for you with my tiny yet powerful halogen spotlight."

In the small spotlight I could see Randee clearly as we crouched. He was a very pale man wearing a red, white, and blue dashiki with a paisley headband. His blond spiky hair stuck straight up from his head. He wore shattered sunglasses and bore an electric guitar strapped to his back. I *think* it was an electric guitar. It was nearly submerged in duct tape.

"What is that thing, man?" said Randee. "One of those bionic TV things? All *right*. Let's watch some tube."

He grabbed it from my hand and pointed it at a broken television in the corner of the dumpster. The screen had a bullet hole in the middle of it.

"This won't work," I said. "That teevee's mortally wounded."

But as Randee switched on the Commander, a pale light began to glow inside the shell of the broken television, like a firefly struggling in a spiderweb. The light grew and took shapes; channels began to switch every five seconds or so, and Destiny Commander began to speak:

5 VIDEO FEEDBACK—

Afternoon Variety; scheduled guests include Nicki Nabob ("Dulles"); Bob Dave ("Dallasty"); singer Vicki Bob.

"Good afternoon, Mr.—er, Randee," said Destiny Commander. "What you are seeing on the monitor is just the tip of the iceberg of my capa—"

"Save the lecture, Destiny," I said. "May I call you Destiny? Des?"

"I have no problem with that, Ian," said Destiny Commander.

"You know, Des," I said. "I like teevee as much as the next potato, but I usually have a working television and outlet when I watch, you get what I'm trying to say?"

"Electricity isn't necessary, Ian," it said. "You only need power for amplification."

> **60** STOCK MARKET
> PUPPETS—
>
> Financial advice for toddlers.

"Amplification of what?" I asked.
"The viewers' random thoughts," said Des.
"Lookit the puppets," said Randee.

> **CNN** WORLD TODAY—
> Yakker/Somber
>
> We sell arms to our enemies,
> then denounce our enemies. Peo-
> ple who question this process are
> called comsymps by White House
> blowhards.

"You mean," I said, "this is a kind of psychological readout of our inmost thoughts?"

"I could be used that way," said Des, "although that wasn't my original function as outlined in Top Secret document SZX 12000. Look at it this way, as dreams come true."

"But this isn't true," I said, waving at the broken TV. "It's just more teevee."

"A television program is a kind of reality," said Des.

"A docudrama of the nation's id?" I asked.

Randee put in his two cents' worth: "The only difference between life and teevee is the size of the box, man. Wouldn't it be great if you could change the world with one of these?"

"That's what I'm trying to tell you," said Destiny. "You aren't being pursued for your money. What they really want is me."

(CINE) MOVIE—
Adventure;
2 hrs

"The Creep" (1980) Half-baked excuse for humor at the expense of fat people and women. Frat Rat: Chubby Chew. Marty: Whiffer Pudgy. Weasel: Guy Dead.

"You?" I asked.

(RANDEE) I LIKE
TRUCKS!—

Randee remembers hitchhiking experiences.

"Hey look! I'm on teevee!"

(SHOALES) IAN IN THE
DUMPS—

In a dumpster behind a Hollywood movie theater, Ian has an intense discussion about the nature of contemporary reality. Ian: Ian Shoales. Guy with no brain cells left: Randee. Remote-control device: Destiny Commander.

"You mean," I asked, "everybody who uses you gets his own network?"

SHOW SIX TWINS FOR
GLORY—

Drama; 60 mns   Episode Six of
this endless miniseries finds Tom
behind Nazi lines, Dick in Moscow, Sally at Pearl Harbor, Jane
in South Africa, Larry coming
down with something, and Mar-
garet attending a White House
func—

"A network of the mind," said Destiny Commander. "The problem
will arise when everybody has a Destiny Commander. That will
mean everyone in America will have his or her dreams, hopes, or
fears airing simultaneously. Reality will gradually be subverted.
Television will encroach on every walk of life. We will no longer
be able to distinguish between programming and living—"

"Turn it off," I said.

kingdom of dreams

"Shh," I said. I could hear, outside the dumpster, the soft crunch of shoes on asphalt.

"God, I hate that," came the voice of Burst.

"Shoes crunching on asphalt?" said Sunder. "I know."

"Quiet, you idiots," came the Fat Man's voice. "I'm trying to
think."

"He's got worries," said Burst.

"Money worries," said Sunder.

"I said, *Shut up*," hissed the Fat Man. I heard the pop of
a gun.

"Ow," said Burst. "What'd you go and shoot me for? Ow.
Ow."

"Shouldn't we take him to a hospital or something?" said
Sunder.

"I put it in the fleshy part of his thigh," said the Fat Man.

"He'll be all right. Mr. Shoales? May I call you Ian, dear boy? I hope you're listening. It's true, we want that money."

"It's a matter of principle," shouted Sunder.

"Quiet," said the Fat Man. "It's not the cash, Ian. Cash is for the poor."

"Sir, ow," said Burst. "Can we get some hydrogen peroxide or something?"

"You may have the money if you can hang on to it," said the Fat Man. "*But* you took a valuable asset of the company—"

"That's me," whispered Destiny.

"—and we mean to have it back. Whatever it takes."

"These are brand-new shoes, sir," said Burst.

"Come on then," said the Fat man. "This way."

Their footsteps went slowly away.

"Oh wow, man," whispered Randee beside me. "Post-Watergate morality."

"We gotta get outta here," I said. "Those people are killers."

"Come on, man," Randee said, "this way."

I pushed aside candy wrappers and styrofoam hamburger containers inside containers, like Chinese boxes, and dug down after Randee.

"I know you, man," he said, throwing a bag of rancid fries over his shoulder. "We went to high school together."

"No we didn't," I said.

"I know we didn't," he said. "But sometimes people think I did, and they give me a dollar so I won't come to the reunion."

"I got a thousand," I said. "If I give it to you, will you go away forever?"

"I had a thousand dollars once," he said. "No, wait, that was *ten* dollars. Once you start adding zeroes, I get confused. That's why I try to avoid money, man, 'cause, like, there's a lot of things more important than money."

"Like what?"

"Well," he said, "gravity. Gravity's real important. Here we are. This is where I live."

We had come to a widening of the corridor, an intersection of conduits. It was a wide cave that echoed with the distant howls of cool air moving underground. I looked around. He had a smoke-damaged futon, a very stiff dog, a microwave oven, and a pile of canned goods.

"You hungry? I could open a can of soup. I don't have a can opener so I use cherry bombs. It's messy but really really effective."

"No thanks," I said. "How do you power those black lights?"

"I got two hamsters on a treadmill, Mailbox and Dirt. I only feed 'em NutraSweet. That keeps 'em going. And that there's my dog Feedback. If I had a pickup I'd put him in the back of it, that's the kind of dog he is, man."

"He looks dead to me."

"I hope so," said Randee. "I had him stuffed two years ago. This place is pretty cool. Of course when it rains, I gotta sleep treading water—"

"How did you know who I was?" I asked.

"I ripped off one of your cassettes," he said.

"Thanks," I said, "I guess. Did you like it?"

"Haven't heard it yet. Haven't been able to score a tape deck."

I noticed the words WAKE UP spray-painted on the wall opposite his bed.

"I gotta get outta here," I said. "There's nine billion dollars out there with my name on it."

"Sure thing. But you better put some clothes on first." He waved a hand at a pile of mildewed clothing piled in a damp corner. "I got my own free box," he said proudly. "Just like the Digger days in the Haight."

I sorted through the pile.

"Better put on three pair of pants," Randee advised.

"Why?"

"In case the first pair catches fire, you got two backup systems."

"My pants have never caught fire," I said.

"You're pushing your luck," he said. "You're living on borrowed time."

I humored him. I put on three pairs of worn corduroys, the wales eroded by countless nervous hands. They hung loosely on me, like the flesh of a weight-watcher after an Herbalife seminar. I put on a white nylon shirt and a jacket with green shields of mold on the elbows, where leather patches might have been.

"You look sharp, man," said Randee. "Kind of like Ward Cleaver with fungus."

"I gotta go," I said.

"Right," said Randee. "Come on, Feedback. Whoops, he fell over. We'll just leave him here, okay? Follow me."

We went down a winding concrete corridor. I noticed a dark figure in a corner.

"Wait a minute," I said, looking closely at the figure. It was the body of a woman, dessicated, starved. "She's dead."

"Yeah, I know," said Randee. "I was gonna write the *Enquirer* about it. I figured if I told 'em she was a movie star or something I could get on the news."

"Right," I said. "Starvation isn't news, but anorexia is. You gotta be rich before people pay attention to your eating habits."

"Keep talkin', man," he said. "I'm hangin' on every word. This is it. Now we gotta climb."

Before us was a vast open space, as large and dark as a looted cathedral. In the middle of this chamber, a mountain of garbage stretched up to a cracked ceiling, then through the crack and beyond. Dark green garbage bags lay like boulders at the base of the mountain. It was a mountain of yellow foam pads, broken chairs, charred mattresses, dolls, television shells, and slashed tires that would never spin again. Through the crack in the ceiling, pale shafts of dusty light struggled down through the gaps; and seepage dripped to the concrete floor. There were dark pools in cracks at my feet, filled with blind trout. Albino alligators stirred in the shadows, as did huge ancient turtles, their backs still showing traces of pink and green paint.

"People flush the weirdest things down the toilet," said Randee. "This is where I got my hamsters. Good thing they can hold their breath."

We pushed aside a rotting mattress, and started to climb.

your top ten countdown
———————————— *images of women in the media*

1. Long-suffering housewife

2. Bitch goddess

3. Wee slip of a thing

4. Bikini bimbo

5. Tireless defender of human rights

6. Good girl gone bad

7. Nurse

8. Nazi lesbian

9. Bitter "other woman"

10. Nancy Drew

tower of babel

"I got a lot of buddies living here," said Randee. He pushed aside a three-legged card table that still held the remains of some half-finished jigsaw puzzle. Behind the card table, in a cubbyhole, sat a frightened woman, clutching a half-empty bottle of screw-top fortified wine. Nobody drinks fortified wine but fraternity boys and skid-row drunks. This woman belonged in the latter category: she had a pooched-out gutter-drinker's stomach, and dragged her wine with her as she backed away into the shadows. In the midst of our national concern about crack, why don't we outlaw that screw-top poison? I guess because winos are just annoying, not thieves. Maybe we're not that worried about crack, really, just about some user with different-colored skin who might liberate our stereo to finance a habit. "Rudy?" this woman asked in a quavering voice. "Is that you? You come back for me, Rudy?"

"He'll be back, Inez," soothed Randee. "It's only been four years. Give the dude time."

He slid the card table back in place, and we resumed our climb.

"She was livin' with this guy Rudy. They was waiting in line to see *The Empire Strikes Back* and he took her money to buy some Olde English and he never come back."

"That's terrible," I said.

"I know, man!" he said. "Those lines are bad. First time I saw one, I said, 'That's weird. A pedestrian traffic jam.' Movies just aren't what they used to be, man, and pedestrians? Forget it."

We kept climbing.

"You gotta go all the way to the Midwest to see true pedestrianism, man, and who's gonna go to the Midwest? Not me. I fly first class, or I don't fly at all, so I don't fly."

"Can we take a break, Randee?" I said.

"Sure," said Randee.

All around us were berths and nooks, like spaces left after a quake in a substandard high rise, or like busted condos after a busted market, scams buried and sunk in the ground, so new scams could build and go bust in the world, so the homeless and hopeless below could live off the dregs of yesterday's fiascoes, live in the rubble of the world's discarded dreams.

"We aren't worthy of our products," said a man's voice. "We are a logo in search of a corporation."

"It's Psycho Boy!" said Randee enthusiastically.

An incredibly filthy man peered from behind a splintered bookcase.

"All your knowledge is useless," he said. He began to walk toward us. The fingernails on his hands had grown to over six inches in length and were sharpened to points. When he smiled I noticed his teeth had been filed to points as well. "The Trilateral Commission has suppressed UFO information," he said.

"Psycho Boy's a genius," whispered Randee in my ear. "But he has this bad habit."

"Just one?" I asked.

"Hey," said Randee. "How many people can say that? And his habit is more of a hobby than a habit."

"What's his hobby?"

"Well, he cuts people into little pieces and mails the pieces to the Phil Donahue Show. He's been pissed at Phil ever since he left Chicago."

"Some hobby," I said.

"He's real good at it though," said Randee. "Hi, Psycho Boy! Please don't kill us, man."

"Your money will kill you," said the wild man, crashing through a barrier of juice bottles. "I will set you free!"

He stretched his arms out and cackled fiercely, his head thrown back.

This guy was starting to get on my nerves.

"Oh, the old root-of-all-evil argument again, huh?" I said. "Well listen, pal, if money is evil, why does my mother send me checks? What are you saying to me, my mother's Hitler?"

"Hitler's in Argentina," said Psycho Boy, creeping closer.

"Your mom's from Argentina?" said Randee.

"You're missing the point," I said.

"I never hit a point in my life," said Randee proudly, ducking as Psycho Boy swiped at his head.

"You don't know what bad is, boy," said Psycho Boy to me. "You ain't never walked a step in the shoes of bad. I got my eye on the eye of God. You got your eye on nothin'."

"Kind of a bitter guy," I said to Randee, backing away. "Isn't he?"

"Gimme that TV thing," said Randee. He took it from my sock, pointed it at Psycho Boy, and turned it on.

Immediately the wild man began to change. His nose elongated. His fingers, already talons, grew longer and sharper. Smoke started to curl from his reddened enlarged nostrils.

"What channel is *this*, brain boy?" I asked.

"Jeeze, I dunno," said Randee. "It reminds me of these dreams I get, ever since that time I took something I probably shouldn't have, and listened to 'Puff The Magic Dragon' about two hundred and seventeen times."

"But what is it?" I asked. It was now about twelve feet high, spewing blue flames from its nostrils, and snapping its jaws in the air. A whimpering noise came from its throat.

"I don't know, man," he said. "But if it ever gets to Honnah Lee, Jackie Paper better not be there. Look, I'm gonna pinch myself or get a wake-up call or something. You can find your way out, can't you?"

I was already on my way.

"You've got a lot of nerve," I shot back over my shoulder. "Coming in my book to hallucinate. Literature is *not* a crash pad."

I was climbing.

On my left, behind a wall of empty hairspray aerosols, two ancient twins marked my passage. They wore reddish ill-fitting wigs, and gave tiny screams as I climbed by. On my right, on a thicket of broken locks, an old man in a jogging outfit lay weeping. I climbed over the car seat of a '57 Studebaker. A drunken couple lay naked on the seat, trying to have sex. The man kept falling off the seat, and the woman was hitting him in the flanks with a gearshift, mumbling "Come on, honey." Her mumbles turned to echoes behind me.

Up I climbed, past dirty children whose faces would never appear on the milk cartons, past squirming bodies and empty cans, past smashed grocery carts filled with pamphlets about Jesuit plots, past visionaries and broken men, past bums and junkies, past the empty and discarded beds, up, finally, into the haze of late-afternoon light.

I pushed aside an empty case of beer littered with discarded condoms, and stood up.

I heard a woman's voice above me.

"Get outta there, ya bum!" she cried, and I felt water wash over me in a flood, like the teardrop of a giant. I looked up to see an angry middle-aged woman with a Miss Piggy haircut. She dangled a dripping bucket, then her face disappeared, and her window slammed shut.

I was standing in a window well, behind an apartment building. I wiped the water off my face and looked around. Looking left, all I could see was the smoldering ruins of a BunniBank, enclosed in barbed wire. On my right, several blocks away, there was a building so tall it broke the clouds. Black clouds shattered at its peak and dissolved into wisps. The building was black glass, as smooth as the face of polished marble. I looked down to the base of the tower to see an awning jutting into the street. L'HOTEL ENNUI was written in script on the awning; next to the awning was a marquee, on which someone had arranged the plastic block words WELCOME IAN SHOALES.

Huh, I thought. *Probably a trap, possibly even a trick of some kind.* I realized Randee still had the Destiny Commander. I remembered Destiny's warning about falling into the wrong hands. Were Randee's hands the wrong hands? Should I go get it back? Climb back down into that darkness? That decay?

Or: Should I brave the probable trap, the possible trick before me? Should I face the hot shower? The stinging shave? The cut of the Giorgio Armani suit which the hotel tailor could no doubt provide?

My choice was clear. I squared my puny shoulders, and resumed walking.

Across the street a sad-eyed Arab wearing a MAGNUM P.I. t-shirt was hammering shut the front door of his storefront. His window was full of Korean imitations of Japanese electronics, and a sign above it all said EVERYTHING MUST GO!

In the doorway of the next storefront, a chunky man in Bermuda shorts was frantically snapping pictures of us. When I met his eyes, he shouted, "Oh! Hiya bud! Say, do you know where I can buy one of those sailor hats with 'Hollywood U.S.A.' written on it? I'm a tourist! I'm from Nebraska!" He was rapidly walking backwards and grinning nervously.

"Everything's closed for the day, pal," I said. "Come back tomorrow."

"We've got him in our sights," came a voice on the other side of the street. Two men in blue suits and Foster Grants put their Florsheims to the pavement and sprinted after the chunky guy, who turned around and began to run. He ran pretty swiftly for a guy his weight. The two guys in blue suits didn't have a prayer of catching him.

A third man stood ten feet away from me, clutching binoculars. When he caught my eye, he grunted and said, "I'm a tourist too. Just an ordinary American citizen." His voice rose in pitch, and cords stood out in his neck. "Listen, if I was employed by the federal government would I be out on the streets like this? No, I'd be pushing paper behind a desk, I'd be filling out forms in triplicate. I'm not on stakeout, sir. I'm just seeing the sights."

He jammed his binoculars against his eyes, and took off running after his companions.

your top ten countdown
images of men in the media

1. Real smoothie
2. Harried husband who needs wise wife to tell him not to wash the whites with the coloreds

3. World-weary spy on one last mission

4. Streetwise cop quick with a wisecrack

5. Stern cop who goes by the book

6. Wise old grandpa

7. Rock star

8. Psycho killer

9. Disturbed Vietnam veteran

10. Madman bent on destroying the world

l'hotel ennui

The lobby of L'Hotel Ennui resembled an enormous kitchen sink—all brushed aluminum and porcelain—with enormous plaster Corinthian pillars set seemingly at random through the space. I marched into the lobby like I owned the joint, which I suppose I had, earlier that morning. Two Latino teenagers dressed like Cossacks rushed to my side.

"Do you have luggage, sir?"

I waved them aside, hoping with this dismissive gesture to indicate that luggage was an idea past its prime. I marched to the front desk and tapped my fingers on the glass countertop until the manager appeared. Get this: the manager was the guy with the blue suit and binoculars I'd just seen on the street! Oh, he'd changed into a salmon-colored blazer, and he had a pink carnation in his lapel; he'd lathered styling gel over his Brylcreem in a shrewd attempt to appear stylish. But he didn't fool me. He wasn't hard to spot. He was still wearing his binoculars, for one thing. He clasped his hands in front of him, gave me a humorless smile, and waited for me to say something.

"Who owns this hotel?" I demanded.

"I don't care," he said. "This is the Hotel Ennui. I know French. I know it's French for 'I don't care.' I'm the hotel manager and I don't care."

I kept tapping my fingers on the glass.

"I'm the hotel manager," he said. Beads of sweat appeared on his forehead. "I'm French. That's my job. The only job I have. What did you think? I work for the feds or something?"

He gave a hearty, loud, and false hoot of laughter, then slammed his hands on the counter. I could see the butt of a weapon in the small cave between the *Miami Vice* label and his Dacron shirt. The distinctive aroma of Paco Rabonne and perspiration drifted my way. Why was he here? Hackles of suspicion rose; the cockles of my heart grew cold.

I turned to the bell captains. "Who owns this hotel?"

They turned to each other.

"Well," said the taller kid, "we were a wholly owned subsidiary of ProCorGenTel this morning, but they got taken over by Fiskel Yahr, the eccentric millionaire, around ten o'clock, but he paid out more cash than he had to buy ProCorGenTel, so now he's selling ProCorGenTel back to the stockholders so he can build up his cash flow. We're waiting for a courier to tell us who owns us now."

"Who cares?" said the manager.

"Do you know the CEO?" I asked.

"This morning it was Ian Shoales. He blew all the assets on videotapes and time machines."

"That's me," I said proudly.

They looked at each other.

"Right," said the short kid. "You're the fast-talking social critic whose acerbic commentaries changed the face of a nation, sure."

"That's me," I insisted.

"I don't care," said the manager. "What suite would you like?"

"Wait a minute," said the short kid. "We can't have impostors checking in here!"

"Why not?" said the manager. "I don't care."

The tall kid threw up his hands when he saw I wasn't going to tip him, and they both wandered away.

"I really didn't care," said the manager. He dangled the platinum key to the penthouse suite in front of my eyes.

"All I have is a thousand bucks," I said.

"Money." He shrugged. "This place hasn't seen cash in years, just plastic. And this morning some joker sucked all the cash out of the city."

He looked at me carefully.

"You know what's happening out there?" he said.

"No," I said. "What?"

"People are hoarding money," he said. "That's against federal law, but I guess they figure it's *collecting*. They figure they're never going to see a buck again. They want to hang on to some, show their kids what it looked like. 'Can I see the picture of Lincoln, Daddy?' 'No son, I'll hang on to *that*. Here, look at this picture of Washington, instead.' 'I like the picture of Lincoln better, Daddy.' "

I made a swipe at the key, but he jerked it back, and frowned at me.

"Ever since we went off the gold standard our economy has gone to hell in a handcart. Know what the new standard is?"

"I don't care," I said.

"That's the spirit!" he said. "The new standard is luck. Every dollar bill is backed by a racehorse. They're off! Where'd they go? You pays your money and you takes your chances. You a Communist, son?"

"My politics are somewhere to the west of middle," I said.

"That's good to hear," he said. "That's a good thing to know. 'Cause you never know what might happen. You never know where a thing like this could end up."

He held the key before him like the head of a victim. He gave me his humorless smile again. I took the key.

"I don't care," he said. "Welcome to Lowtel Onwee. I hope your stay with us will be a pleasant one."

the best room in the house

The door was as thick as a Manhattan phone book; it opened noiselessly on well-oiled hinges. I stood for a moment in the doorway and gaped at the suite spread out before me. A little sunken living room nestled snugly against the curtained window, which took up the entire wall. The lavender couch looked just right for two. On my left was a television as large as a refrigerator, and a refrigerator as large as a television. Both were bolted to the floor, of course, but the bolts were *very* tasteful, pastel bolts of sturdy ABS, from By Design. On my right, the bed—hard, wide, and inviting as a parlor. The gray flannel sheets were turned back, and on the pillow were a daisy and a chocolate.

I stepped into the room, and immediately sank to my ankles in the rich pile. I waded through the carpet to the closet. There were those little shoe-bags, of course, which no fine hotel can be without, and a wet bar, and another television, no larger than a shoebox. I waded to the bathroom to find *dozens* of enormous towels, a magazine rack and bookshelf, stocked with every current issue and each book from *The New York Times* best-seller list, *hardcover!* And L'Hotel Ennui didn't mess around with those tiny little sampler bottles of toiletries, no, they provided *gallon jugs* of name-brand shampoo, hair rinse, and mouthwash. They provided a tube of imported toothpaste as big as a log. Instead of a mirror, L'Hotel Ennui had a video camera and monitor. So when you shaved, you could see yourself on television, the way you *should* be seen, not unnaturally reversed.

Behind the shower curtain, I found a bathtub as large as a pool at the Y, with not one, but *three* pulsating massage shower heads. Another television had been installed in the ceiling; and a telephone, telex, and photocopy machine were neatly tucked in a nook under the sterling silver Hot and Cold nozzles.

Going back into the bedroom again, I found a remote-control unit. It wasn't Destiny Commander, but it was the next best thing. One button made the bed vibrate gently. I pushed another and hidden doors on each side of the bed slid silently open. I walked through the doorway on the right to find an Olympic-size swimming pool; a whirlpool, sauna, and tennis court were revealed, with a mini-mall at the far end, *sure* to make available my every traveling need. A distant clerk sent me a friendly wave.

I waded through the carpet to the second doorway, which opened onto an exact replica of Fiskel Yahr's apartment! There was the home entertainment center, there the scrawled WAKE UP! I could hear the discreet whir of *Time Chopper Twelve* on the other side of the window, monitoring my sleeping thoughts from my happy future, and there, on the downy futon, there even seemed to be a figure sleeping. The staff at L'Hotel Ennui had worked fast and overtime to create this masterful illusion. There was the television spinning its dial, there was even that distant buzzing, the suggestion of earsplitting clangor and alarm. They'd added the clever detail of some neighbor pounding at the front door. You can almost hear his muffled shouts. There! Hear it? "Turn off your alarm! You're waking up the neighborhood, you sonofabitch!" I chuckled to myself and closed the door on the realistic scene.

Pointing my remote-control at the window, the silk curtains slithered apart to reveal enormous black clouds moving ponderously by, and between the clouds, the city of angels lay before me, as if seen from a jet plane hanging fire in the sky. The smoldering ashes of BunniBanks still were faint red dots scattered across the cityscape. Strange. They seemed almost to spell out words against the encroaching darkness: "W-A-K-E-U-"—but that was impossible. Merely an illusion, that's all.

A pair of powerful Zeitgeist binoculars hung in a handsome leather stirrup on the arm of the couch. I cracked a cold malt liquor (L'Hotel Ennui had anticipated my every need!) and scanned the city below for signs of my besieged money.

There! In that parking lot. A tight circle of limousines. I adjusted my focus. I could see thousands of people swarming like ants on the limos. Even from this distance, their needs were as naked as a newborn child. Clever Sarge! He'd made a protective shell of the briefcases. Through chinks in that makeshift armor, I could make out the drivers, sitting cross-legged in a circle, playing poker. With *my* money.

Suddenly annoyed, I pulled the Touch-Tone over, and fingered the number of Sarge's cellular phone. In seconds I heard his smooth attentive voice.

"ShoalesCo," he said cheerfully, "the company with a heart. May I help you?"

"It's me," I said.

"The boss!" he shouted back to the others. Through the binoculars, I saw the card game break up and the drivers scurry to their vehicles. "Where are you?"

"In the penthouse suite at L'Hotel Ennui," I said.

"Where? Oh yeah. Hey, I can see you looking at me through the window! Hi Ian! Can you see me wave?"

"Cut that out, Sarge. What's the situation?"

"They haven't been using their weapons. I guess they don't have cash for bullets. The limos are all bulletproof anyway. They've been bombarding us with canned goods—"

"How long can you hold out?" I interrupted.

"Weeks if we had to," he said. "The limos are all stocked with paté. What's the plan?"

"The plan?" I asked. "Oh yeah, I've got a plan. Don't worry. I'll get you out of there. Give me a half hour or so to freshen up."

"Check," said Sarge. I hung up the phone and slumped on the couch. What a day. I'd tramped through its narrows and deeps, its fires and damps, leaving opinions in my churning wake, the cast-off debris of a drifter on a roll. I am the doctor with the tough pills, I am the soldier with the smoking gun, I am the hammer at the cold stone wall. But I'd twisted too many similes, got up way too early, and my own thoughts exhausted me. *Must I have an opinion on everything? Can't I just let things be?*

I called Room Service.

"What you need," said the sultry voice, "baby I got it."

"I need a swell Italian suit," I said, "and socks. And, uh, I probably need some help."

"Whom do you wish to summon, Seeker?"

"I don't know," I said. "Read my aura, if I've got one, give me a half hour or so, and send somebody up. Somebody spiritual, you know?"

"Your wish is our command," said the voice.

We disconnected. This was my kind of hotel. The sun hung, like an advertisement for sunset, in the sky. The curtain whispered shut with the push of a button. The long night stretched before me, and at its end, I hoped, Ruth.

I took off my clothes, put on the terrycloth robe the hotel had provided, and spun the dial.

46 GRAFFITI!—

Mugging. Tattooed teens explain the symbols to you, then
rob you at knifepoint.

If what Destiny Commander had told me was true, every hand
controlling Destiny was a hand controlling the dreams of America.
Therefore, the street-life dreams of Randee and his friends would
spread like wildfire: a kind of video virus.

So far, Destiny's programming didn't look that different from
regular programming. If this was chaos and anarchy, at least it was
chaos and anarchy that reflected the way some people live, not the
chaos and anarchy of your typical TV producer's brain.

CNN WARY THING—

Talk; 60 mns. Wary's guest is
trance channeler Conceptula La
Boola Boola. Dead people answer
stupid questions.

Still, I supposed it was up to me to do something. The problem
seemed to be too many choices, too much freedom. Maybe I needed
to take Destiny to a place where freedom has never shone. Total
freedom means totalitarianism? The devil and the deep blue sea?
The rock and the hard place? The irresistible force and the immov-
able object? Would this be a cure or a curse?

I dunno.

C SPAN

Congressmen discuss fastest
ways to get to airports.

I just don't know.

Is this thing a problem or a solution?

Should I worry that television and life are gradually becoming
the same thing, or should I just flow with it?

And what if a television program took over *this book?* My publishers would really be— hey, wait a minute. That woman on MTV
looks familiar. Let me turn up the sound and hear what the veejay
is saying . . .

VEEJAY

. . . a major crush, huh?

RUTH

This guy in my mythology class. I batted my eyes blind, but
he didn't tumble to my charms. So I threw Ovid away, dropped
out of school, and went into music full-time.

VEEJAY

His loss is our gain.

RUTH

That's certainly an oily way to put it.

VEEJAY

Ha ha. Ruth has a brand-new album on the brand-new Destiny
label, which I understand is one of many assets up for grabs
in the big ProCorGenTel shake-up. The album is called *Fire
and Money*, and she'll be appearing *tonight* at Monroe's Doctrine, a new club in Moscow, North Dakota. Hope to see some

of you jet-setters there. Thanks for the chat, Ruth, and let's check out her new video, "Operator," coming at ya, through the miracle of satellite transmission, right now.

future perfect

I still remember 1988. The Sexual Revolution was over at last. All across the country, bodies lay in ruins. The temple of the flesh had fallen, and desire tucked its head, like a turtle besieged. Gay men didn't know their pleasure had a price; how could they? All talk was of morality and freedom, none of information. So the love that dared not speak its name was once more as nameless as dread. The closets filled up again, while moral fools pounded on the doors to jeer, "I told you so!"

Awkwardness replaced flirtation. Fear stalked the sexual stomping grounds. Poor black girls, unmarried, with children, were hounded by media hounds in search of problems which made good video. And all people wanted was a little love in their lives, and they didn't care what it cost. They didn't know the price. Donahue watchdogs snapped at the heels of the sexy. Uninformed idiots barred children with AIDS from school as though orgies and needle-sharing were common kindergarten activities. America became filled with people who thought sexual disease was like household dust, and only Pledge and God could keep deadly sin from smudging their mealy lives.

That's when I stepped in. I knew there was no need to throw out the bathwater of love, just because there was a baby in it. I introduced the Sex Mom, as discreet as she was plump, as wise as she was healthy, as big-hearted as she was cautious. Her motto: *Enjoy your body, but don't leave your brain at home.* She did what you were too self-conscious to do. A qualified nurse, she examined the records of potential partners. She examined your potential partners. She examined you. There was no need to be shy around her. She'd seen it all before.

She helped you disrobe, if that's what you wanted, she slipped on the condom with expert indifferent hands. She soothed fears with statistics and pamphlets. And while you sought your pleasure, she was right outside the door with her knitting and magazines. And when you were spent in the aftermath of desire, she brought you a glass of water, or a moist towelette. She'd tuck you in, read you a story, turn on the night-light.

I launched a fleet of Sex Moms. They made me rich. They allowed me to indulge my whims. My Perfect World of Wax.

To showcase that Perfect, fleeting moment in 1988 when Ian Shoales first glimpsed his/my beloved Ruth, the Perfect World of Wax created the Hall of Lost Things. The fact that his/my loving glimpse was of her on a television music video need not diminish the poignancy of that moment. And it will not, has not. Not here.

Here the banks of rhinestone-bedecked monitors play Ruth's video continuously. Below the screens, on that vast slab of granite, the lyrics to her song have been carved deep into the stone.

We have provided two entranceways to the Hall of Lost Things, for men and women. No couples may pass through those portals, singles only single file, no touching, no food or talking, no flashbulbs or recordings, keep it moving, enjoy yourselves.

On a television screen in a Hollywood hotel room, Ian first saw her. Her song was called "Operator." On the video, frozen, we see the product information on the lower left of the screen, another dying gasp of the printed word. Who watches television to *read?* We read:

RUTH
"Operator"
FIRE AND MONEY
Destiny

Above that, there's the still face of Ruth herself, her full lips about to smile. She has an ultra-light headset on her head. She sits behind a semicircle of telephone lines, and she gazes at the camera with an expectant look, as if she's about to reveal an amazing television offer.

Let's roll the tape. Follow the bouncing LazerBall™ as it touches the granite:

You've been using bad connections (she sings)
But it's too late for the blues.
You knew how to clean your life out,
But what you kept you couldn't use.

I know the nature of your problem.
I've seen the poison and the fire.
As the city sleeps I am standing by.
I'm here to anchor down the wires.
I'm here for you.

Fiber-optic snakes twist around her like the hair of Medusa. Yet stone hearts melt at the sight of her. Messages of light halo her hair. Lines of light pass through her switchboard. She's the center of strings of light, as calls catch fire around her. And as she sings, she sprouts wings, and those wings are light.

You've been thrown against your ego,
Like a spy against the wall.
Every thought's a firing squad
Just before the fall.

You might be a fallen angel
Or an ape that learned to fly,
But the light from a distant broken star
Still shines up in the sky.
I see it shine!

And she begins to rise, to levitate. Her vast wings carry her away. The walls of the cold office vanish. The room vanishes. The window disappears and she is already flying into the universe, a tiny figure lost among the stars, vanishing.

This is hard to do in real life. Real life is harder and less dangerous than television.

Ruth. Oh, if I'd known her when. I could have come singing over the wires. I could have placed a pure voice in her voice-weary ears—the voice of Marlowe to a dame he liked, the voice of Bonnie Raitt at two A.M., the voice of an angel to a frightened child—but alas, kids, that voice I no longer have.

Gone: the extremes of dreams, the honor of offers, the glow of the gone day on smooth skin, the beauty of duty, the truth of youth, the misses mister kissed, the kisses missed, kids, are gone from me, gone.

I want to erase every corrupted wisdom and fly away with her, to a cottage by the fire, where little Fawn and Ollie frolic in the dew. Because what I'm left with, here in the future, is a boyish appeal grown a little wizened. I'm left with a world where the tricks I did don't do the trick anymore. I live with the consequence of desire, with the snakes and heebie jeebies, where everybody's a jump ahead of a fit, with nothing to show for the living of life but mixed emotions and a wicked world. She vanishes. The screen grows black.

And the men and women emerge from the Hall of Lost Things, shaken, blinking in the sudden sunlight, groping toward the light of day, searching for some hand to hold, even the hand of a stranger.

Switch the channel.

(WTBS) (6:03) MOVIE—

Elvis; 1 hr 39 mns. "Speedway Karate" (1961)   Elvis walks through this lame excuse for a movie, his eyes staring off-camera, as though there were some better world beyond the frame, where simple people gather and sing, where freight trains and hound dogs moan at night, where crickets and porches creak in rhythm, where a man can dream the sweet dreams of a good sleep, and never dread the morrow. He gets the girl, and saves his world. Mary Ann Mobley. Elvis Presley.

Ian takes a cold shower at
L'Hotel Ennui. Language, nudity, not recommended for children under seventeen. Let's give
it a rest. Let's turn the damn
thing off.

Let's get out of here.

your top ten countdown
———————————— *top ten ideas that shaped the
modern world*

1. *Deconstruction* Everything is a signal. Nothing means what
   you think it means. Before you cross that street on the green
   light, you have to consider the idea of "green," the history
   of streets, and discard the antithesis: "red." Art is anthro-
   pology. Outmoded concepts (such as artists' intentions) no
   longer obtain. This means you can actually study comic
   books in college, and nobody will laugh at you! It means
   your reaction is more important than what you are reacting
   to. Previously, a viewer of art was put smack in the middle
   of the artistic process, like Lucky Pierre. Now, the viewer
   is a Peeping Tom on his or her own thoughts.

2. *Minimalism* An inadvertent by-product of structuralism.
   Embarrassed by the history of their chosen media, and by
   a perceived "exhaustion" of images and stories, artists,
   like turtles, drew into their shells, shaved their heads, and
   emerged as kind of downtown monks, chanting "Less is
   more." Click tracks, drum machines, clear true lines, video,
   cordless mikes, ostinato.

3. *Post-Industrialism* Bye-bye, steel. Bye-bye, working man.

4. **Demographics/statistics** Powerful tools, used selectively by the powerful to reinforce plans they were going to make anyway. Vietnam, This Whole Iran Thing, exit polls, phone polls, terms like *Baby Boomers, AOR, MOR, upwardly mobile,* and *homeless* are statistical constructs, and are only of use in the gathering of funds. A smattering of statistics makes any report look good.

5. **Neo-Sexuality** Perfume commercials and bad sex—is that what the Sexual Revolution gave us? Is sex divorced of consequence? Another spectator sport, and a rigged one at that, like professional wrestling? Is sex only interesting if you're a participant? Is pornography a disguise for confusion? Do we really need *fantasies* to masturbate? I don't know. Just asking.

6. **Post-Modernism** This word only means something if you know what modernism is. Taken by itself it means something like "after now." Sometimes I think language isn't a tool at all, but a weapon. We use it to ambush those who think differently than we do. Artists invent terms like *post-modernism* so they can either moonlight as critics, or create a marketplace for their art by creating a genre for it. More power to them (and critics as well), but it does prove that art has a shelf life like anything else. Like bread. Bread can be art, if you put your name on it, and put it in a gallery. Make sure your name's on it though. Without the irony and quotation marks around it, it's just something else to eat.

7. **Geopolitics** *Realpolitik* charters a plane. Machiavelli gets a passport. Oliver North chokes up for the camera. Gorbachev hires a public-relations expert. Has there ever been a study done to show the effects of jet lag on diplomatic relations?

8. **Video** Each duplication of a video is called a *generation*. Each generation grows paler and paler, until it's just a static-ridden ghost of the original. Digital recording will change all that. There will be no such thing as "original" and "copy." Nothing will be lost, and nothing gained—a parody of in-

finity. When you crank up digital sound, you don't hear any tape hiss! All of human history and innovation has led to the lack of tape hiss. I tell you, it sends shivers up my spine every time I don't hear it.

9. **_Neo-Economics_**   Spend now. Pay later. Have trouble understanding? Try this simple test: You are a fund-raiser for a Washington lobby. You receive a ten-thousand-dollar donation from a bored Republican in Texas. You wire this money to Panama, where it is deposited in the accounts of two corporate fronts, transferred to the Bahamas, then to a Swiss bank account, then to Liechtenstein, then back to D.C. to the accounts of the Young Admirers of Imaginary Traditions, who distribute autographed photographs of Presidents and helicopters to bored wealthy Republicans in exchange for ten-thousand-dollar donations. What do you call this process? Answer: More than a lifestyle, it's a new American way of life.

10. **_Communism_**   Workers and students just don't get along. It's taken us awhile to figure this out. Communism doesn't work, but its death throes are mind-boggling.

Now this.

perfect pitch
———————————— Commercial; 60 seconds
(CONVERGENCE AIRLINES)

VIDEO	AUDIO
A SLEEK SILVER AIRPLANE HANGS IN A SILVER SKY. IT BLURS AT THE EDGES, THEN ZOOMS OUT OF FRAME.	CHORUS OF VOICES Arise! Arise and fly! FX: SONIC BOOM

EMPTY SILVER SKY

ANNOUNCER
You can hurtle through time and space at incredible speeds.

CUT TO:

A SLEEK SILVER AIRPLANE HANGS IN A SILVER SKY, MOTIONLESS.

Or you can take your time.
FX: WHISTLING WIND

At Convergence Airlines, the choice is yours.

CUT TO:

INTERIOR OF SLEEK AIRPLANE, PASSENGERS STRAPPED IN, FACES COTORTED FROM THE PULL OF MANY G-FORCES.

New York to Paris in five minutes.

CUT TO:

INTERIOR OF SLEEK AIRPLANE. THE WINDOWS ARE OPEN. PAS-SENGERS ARE LEANING OUT. SOME ARE WAVING TO PEOPLE FAR BELOW.

ANNOUNCER
Or New York to Paris in five days.

At Convergence Airlines, the choice is yours.

CUT TO:

ATTRACTIVE FLIGHT ATTEN-DANT READING A THICK NOVEL. PASSENGER AP-PROACHES. FLIGHT ATTENDANT DOESN'T LOOK UP.

We won't pamper you.

PASSENGER
Can I get a cup of coffee?

FLIGHT ATTENDANT
Go ahead. I'm not your ser-vant, sir. I'm a trained professional.

116

CUT TO:

OPEN WINDOW. A PASSENGER LEANS TOO FAR OUT AND FALLS. A SECOND PASSENGER GRABS A FLIGHT ATTENDANT.

ANNOUNCER
At Convergence Airlines, every choice is yours.

SECOND PASSENGER
Miss, that man fell out the window!

FLIGHT ATTENDANT
He was an adult, who chose not to wear his seat belt. You must live with the choices you make in life. Or die with them. The choice is always yours.

SLEEK SILVER PLANE HANGING FIRE IN THE SKY.

ANNOUNCER
Dance on the wing under the stars or cling to your seat for dear life. At Convergence, you make the choices. Don't blame us. Try us.

CHORUS OF VOICES
Arise! Arise and fly with me!

ANNOUNCER:

Ian will be back after these brief messages.

your top ten countdown

bottom ten ideas that shaped the modern world

1. ***Eschatology***   You could look it up, I suppose, but then again, why bother?

2. ***Poetics***   There's a fine line between art and communication.

Poetry today avoids both those lines, and contents itself with petty academic squabbles.

3. *Hermetics*   How many alchemists do *you* know?

4. *Narrative*   Has been replaced by scenarios and slices of life.

5. *Iconography*   Has been replaced by trademark searches.

6. *Psychology*   Came and went pretty fast, really.

7. *Surrealism*   Survives as an adjective.

8. *Expressionism*   Passed like a cold breeze.

9. *Charity*   Survives in corners of society, with no official support.

10. *Hope*   Has been replaced by misguided certainty.

PART FOUR

Night

in which we hit the road

Food for Thought

. . . you were kicked by a great man, and with a beautiful
ivory leg, Stubb. It's an honor; I consider it an honor.

> —Herman Melville, *Moby Dick*

He as soon chop a chile in two as a cat.
—Jim (on the wisdom of Solomon)

> —Mark Twain, *The Adventures of Huckleberry Finn*

My life is good.

> —Randy Newman, "My Life is Good"

And there I saw the dark imaginings
Of felony, the stratagems of kings

> —Chaucer, "Knight's Tale," *Canterbury Tales*

mister em dee what's ailing me?

In the penthouse suite at L'Hotel Ennui, I vigorously toweled my damp hair and thought: *You'd think I'd have learned, love-wise, what makes people tick. I've had enough experience.* My last girlfriend (Number Thirty, name withheld to protect her innocence) slammed the door behind her. I can still hear those quick angry footsteps down the hall. The trouble is, Honesty is my middle name. I'd told her from the start I was a jerk, but she didn't believe me. Maybe she thought I was being ironic.

It probably didn't help that every time she used the word *relationship* I would cover my ears and go "laylerlaylerlayler." I was trying to be playful. I was trying to awaken the child in me. I was trying to suggest to her that the word *relationship* best refers to the connection between parasite and host, or shark and remora. It's a biological term. I'd rather be a jerk than a scientist when it comes to love.

Number Thirty tried. She made me watch *Purple Rose of Cairo* (good movie, I admit). She made me read Raymond Carver, the poet of the trailer parks. But then, emboldened by her success, she began to bring me books by psychologists and single fathers and divorced women; confessionals and slim novels; books by survivors and the Engineers of the New Success; *best-sellers.* I tried my best, believe me, but halfway through *Smart Women, Foolish Choices,* something snapped.

I remember I was standing by the fireplace when she returned home and confronted me, perhaps because I was using her books for firewood. I was basking in the glow of *Bright Lights, Big City* when she said, "What do you think you're doing?"

I said: "I'm putting this yuppie Thomas Mann to some practical use."

She was silent for a moment, then she began straightening things. When a woman starts to straighten things, it's always Uh-Oh Time. She began to speak in that low even tone women get when they're that special kind of angry. "All you think about is yourself," she said. Women are so good at this. She said, "You don't know what love is" and "You have no respect for my needs" and "You think life is a movie." She said, "You don't deserve a relationsh—"

I didn't hear the rest because I had my hands over my ears and I was going "laylerlaylerlaylerlayler." I kept it up until I heard the front door slam, then I said, "Well, I did it again" to nobody, threw *Elvis and Me* on the fire, and thought about what she'd said.

All you think about is yourself. Well yeah. Who doesn't? That's why we look for love, to bring us out into the world. I want someone to hoot with me at Nancy Reagan's clothing, someone who shares my amusement with Lyndon LaRouche's political theories, someone who avoids the word *lifestyle,* and doesn't use *impact* as a verb, someone who appreciates my opinions but considers the personality from whence they came, and doesn't put the thought before the source: someone, in short, who doesn't take me as seriously as I do.

You don't know what love is. I know what love is: Tracy and Hepburn and Bogart and Bacall and Romeo and Juliet and Jackie and John and Marilyn and Heloise and Abelard and Dante and Beatrice: doomed love, teen love, endless love, love iconified: DiMaggio's flowers on Norma Jean's grave. Who can compete with that?

But despite the fear and demographics and diet plans, the Monster From the Id (*Forbidden Planet,* 1956) is still an animating ghost. We are still haunted by the urge to cry, "My darling, my truth, my rock, my pudding, my shoe!" Love is never what we looked for and always takes us by surprise: it's the rock on Coyote's head in the middle of the Road Runner chase. It's not the pain of love Coyote minds, it's the futility of his inventions in the face of his fate.

You have no respect for my needs. Okay, I realize that when I say "I love you" you want me to say it like Cary, not Groucho. I accept that. Women like sincerity in a man. But you gotta remember, some lines just stick in my craw: "That's a great haircut," "I'd *love* to play Trivial Pursuit," "I'd *love* to hear the other side." I like kisses and gazes as much as the next guy, but I can't go around murmuring "My rock, my pudding, my shoe" all the time. I'd feel like a sap.

You think life is a movie. I wish it was. I'd prefer the movie to my life. I could fast-forward through the dull parts, and time-shift the cool parts to view at my convenience. I could preface the movie with words of caution: *Viewer Discretion Advised, Adult Situations, Language, Nudity.* Here, Number Thirty, you can play yourself. I know you're out there. You bought this book to see what I'd say about you. We'll get a young Cassavetes to play me. He throws Richard Gere on the roaring fire and reaches for your hand. Let's freeze that frame (looks like a liqueur ad in *The New Yorker*, doesn't it?) and remember: a romance that ends happily is not a romance. Let's rewind to 1970 to prove this point.

There's a close-up of Girlfriend Number Four (played by a complete unknown whom we will generously set on the road to stardom). How young she looks as she turns and walks away. Track her as she SloMoes down the stairs. (A Beatles song fills the sound-track, with a kettledrum counterpoint to indicate the threat of far-away war). She steps outside into that movie snow. Diamonds melt on her tear-stained cheeks. The camera is swooning. Empathy occurs. Popcorn crunches like bones in the darkness. *(We need a song by Joni Mitchell here, J.B., or James Taylor, the hippie Perry Como.)*

Pull back to reveal my distant face in an upstairs window. Cut to: POV Ian, as I watch her trudge away forever. We see her superimposed face in the sky, as large as a house, laughing at a joke I told, months before. It's over. In a lap-dissolve we replace her face with mine, as I gain years and dark circles and lines and girlfriends (and a song by UB40; "Please Don't Make Me Cry" would be appropriate) as I watch Number Thirty stride furiously down the street. It would only be a matter of seconds before she remembered: this was her apartment, not mine. And I'd be gone again. Gone.

Yes, a movie would capture all the dumb kids, whose ideas of love were learned from magazines and movies and songs, who grew up stupefied by their own emotions. If life was a movie, I would have learned something by now.

You don't deserve a relationsh— Probably not. After Girlfriend Four left me, I went to see *Love Story*; when Ryan O'Neal pushed aside Ali McGraw's tubes to share a kiss, I screamed at the screen and had to be evicted forcibly. After Girlfriend Thirty it was *Commando*. I didn't even have the energy to hoot. I barely had the energy to intimidate the box office into giving me my money back. I skulked back to my studio like a whipped puppy, where Fiskel Yahr's message awaited me: the L.A. gig was on.

So there I was, high in a penthouse suite in L'Hotel Ennui, spinning the dial. Who am I supposed to be attracted to in this silly culture? That excited woman waxing a shiny surface? No. That woman with capped teeth and terrifying hairdo? No. That slim shirtless woman with puckered lips, circling a gawking boy? No. Obviously phony. There's nothing I hate worse than a phony pucker. There's Dr. Ruth. Ruth, should I find my Ruth? Doctor, should I pursue? Is it healthy, Doctor, to hold hands in the darkness and watch the movie stars kiss, their heads as large as boulders? Doctor, how can our kiss compare with those kissing mountains? Give me a sweet nothing, Doctor, to whisper in her ear. Doctor says, "Love is a dream, that's all, and we hope we don't awaken, but the lights come up and the bored ushers swing wide the doors, and we spill out dazed and lonely into the streets full of criminals and fools, and the distant drums of faraway wars—" and there's Della Street, my first love. She can dial a telephone with a pencil. I admire that in a woman. And there's the door. Who could it be? I began to wade through the carpet to answer it.

the proper authorities

The door swung open before I could touch it. Five feet away, a little wiry guy stood, wearing black chinos, black t-shirt, and a black leather jacket. He had one hand jammed in his rear pocket, and the other dangled a room key between whitened thumb and forefinger.

"The clerk let me borrow this," he said. His sunglasses wobbled on his nose. "He said he didn't care. So what did you think?"

"About what?"

"About Ruth's *video*, man, what else? Don't tell me you didn't watch it. Ruthie needs to know if you're going to push the album or sit on it. We've still got a contract with you people, you know.

If you'd sit still long enough, stop the corporate maneuvers, maybe we could figure out who we've got a contract *with*, you follow me? Who's in charge, man? Who's minding the store? Do you want Ruthie or not? She's a valuable asset for you. We've got the material, we've got the band together. We're ready to sign a three-album deal with you, but if you don't want it, say it now, we'll shop around. You know Gordy?"

"Gordy?" I asked. I started to wade toward him again. This twerp talked almost as fast as I did.

"Gordy," he said. "Gordy! A and R at Falcon Records. He's got a package offer for us, but frankly we want your film options."

"Ruth wants to act?" I asked. Rock stars think it's easy to make that leap from video to celluloid. I suppose it is for *them*, but the hills are full of *real* actors who wait tables while rock stars dabble. I tell you, folks, it's a hell of a world.

"Who knows what she wants," he said. "I just don't want to close off that option. We're loose. We're ready. Can I come in?"

"No," I said.

"Thank you, thank you," he said, coming in and closing the door behind him. "Thank you. Christ, this carpet's deep, so what did you think?"

"I liked the song," I said. "The video sucked. I only put it in the book because Ruth was in it, and I thought having a music video in a work of fiction would be some kind of first."

"We can reshoot it if you didn't like it," he said. He tried to grab my arm in a sincere gesture, but missed, and fell over.

"You can't move too fast in this pile," I said.

"I lost my sunglasses," he said. "Frankie Goes to Hollywood. They had to do a zillion different videos of that song before people finally paid attention. What was that song?"

"Look, pal," I said. "I gotta get dressed. I gotta find the woman I love, I gotta save the world, probably—"

"Don't go," he said. "Oh God, not yet. Come see her at least. Come see her tonight. Moscow, North Dakota. Take the red-eye on Convergence, they go so fast, you'd be there before you left almost. You'd get there before the first set, it's *hot* I'm tellin' ya. It's all coming together, you're the only piece that's missing. Here they are."

He had his arm into the carpet up to his elbow. He withdrew his arm with his sunglasses in his fist. He struggled to rise.

"Wait a minute," I said. "Who are you, and who do you think I am?"

"I'm Hank," he said. "I got a card somewhere. I'm Ruth's manager, or I was until she signed with Destiny. But will Destiny give her their full attention the way I have for three years? Sure, she hasn't signed any deal since she signed with me, but is that my fault? It's the world's fault, man. It's people like you, admit it, come on, *come on*. Do you think I buy all this 'Sat-Next-to-Me-in-My-Mythology-Class' bullshit? This love from afar? I think you and Ruthie made some kind of private deal—that's okay!" He held up a hand. "That's okay. Circles in circles, you know, the joke's on me, but I'm Ruthie's manager, I need to know! Am I cut out, do I get a percentage, what's the deal?"

"*Who* do you think I am?" I asked.

"Fiskel Yahr," he said.

"I'm Ian Shoales," I said.

"Come on, man, don't shine me with that social-critic crap. That opinion-making stuff is an East Coast scam. This is L.A. and you're the man with a plan."

"Okay," I said. "What's my plan?"

"I'm a manager, man, not a mogul! All I know is, you bought this company and this company's got Destiny, and Destiny just signed Hat Band, and Hat Band needs a single to open for them, and that's *Ruthie*, Mr. Yahr Fiskel! I don't know if you follow the music scene or if you got people who do, but you're making the right moves, and I want to move with it. I'm hungry! I'm young! I've seen the portfolios, I follow the market, I've seen your catalogs!"

He'd been ticking off points, and he ran out of fingers. He looked at me shrewdly.

"I'm not Fiskel Yahr," I said.

"I know the M.O.!" he screamed. "Okay." He settled down and took a deep breath. "Okay. Ian. Can I call you Ian, Ian? Okay, Ian, now that I know who you really are, Ian, come on, it'll be our little secret, Ian, your little con, Ian, now you owe me something, man, you stole my act right out from under me! She was the last act I had! She was the only act I ever had!"

"Get outta here," I said. "I want to get dressed."

"Right," he said, disgusted. "And what's the next line? 'I'll call you, Hank, I'll see you.' 'I'll see you.' That is the whole gestalt right there. Isn't that the whole pattern though? *I'll see you, I'll see you*, and nobody ever sees me. I might as well be invisible. 'We'll get back to you, Hank,' but nobody *ever sees me!*"

He made a mighty lurch with his body, freeing himself from the clutches of the carpet, and seized my leg.

"Okay, okay!" he shouted. "I don't know who you are! I'm speaking for Ruth, you know. Talk to me! We're adults! We're not kids! I don't care if you hate me! I love my work! Just let me do my work!"

"Christ," I muttered. I was trying to trudge through the carpet to the door, dragging this occupational burnout on my leg. All the money in the world couldn't recompense me for moments like this.

"She doesn't need you," he babbled. "*We* don't need you. She doesn't remember you. I never heard her talk about you. I've never heard *anybody* talk about you. You're doomed to failure, Mr. Fiskel, can I call you Ian? You loser! I love you!"

I had my hand on the door, when it opened again.

There, to my relative dismay, stood my untiring pursuers, Burst, Sunder, and the Fat Man. The Fat Man had disguised himself as the chunky guy I'd seen on the street (page 100, if you've forgotten). He was still wearing his Bermuda shorts and holding a camera. As I recalled he'd been chased by the feds. What did the feds want with him? He beamed at me, and said:

"Talk yourself out of this one, smart guy."

Burst was on crutches and looked unhappy. Sunder had something large and unwieldy under his sports coat. He cast furtive glances both ways down the hallway, and struggled to remove the bulky object. It was a high-powered rifle. It slipped through his fingers and fell, hitting Burst's crutches. Burst fell over.

"Hey, watch it," said Burst.

"You watch it," said Sunder. "This is the last gun we got."

"Record producers?" panted Hank, still clasping my leg.

"These guys don't produce anything," I said. "They just skim profits from the stream."

"And you can't fish in a dead stream," said the Fat Man. He

smiled at me and then, in one smooth motion, removed his own head (an *amazing* special makeup effect, by the way, a miracle of latex and tubing; if books could get special Oscars, believe me, this head would qualify), revealing the small furry head of Fiskel Yahr, maverick, raider, greenmail expert. "Unzip me, Mr. Sunder," he said. As the rest of the Fat Man's bloated body fell away, Fiskel talked to me. "When I was a kid," he said, "I used to sit on a hill, and wish they'd drop the big one, just so I could sit on that hill, and watch it all come down. I wouldn't mind going, just so I'd be the last one to go. You ever have those fantasies, Ian?"

"*That's* Fiskel Yahr," I told Hank. "Sic 'em."

Hank dropped my leg like a hot potato, and crawled to the doorway, rummaging through his pockets as he wallowed forward. "I got a card here somewhere—"

"Snowshoes," Fiskel said, snapping his fingers. Sunder helped Burst to his feet, then removed the pair of snowshoes strapped to Fiskel's back. *Clever,* I thought. *Wearing those snowshoes, Fiskel can just slide across the surface of the carpet.* Hank, meanwhile, had leaped from the room and seized Fiskel's leg.

"My card!" he screamed. He held Fiskel's leg with one arm, and held his business card upstretched with the other.

"And which one are you?" asked Fiskel, looking at the card indifferently. "Murray or Murray?"

"I'm Hank. Murray and Murray retired. One word, Fiskel, one word. Ruth D."

"That's two words," said Fiskel. Burst had limped over to him. He inserted the tip of a crutch between Hank's fingers and Fiskel's leg, and was prying them off one by one.

I didn't have much time. I threw myself onto the carpet, and started to swim. If I could just make it to Door Number Two, if I could just wake up from this foolish dream—! I cursed myself for giving up those swimming lessons when I was ten. Though I was dog-paddling furiously, I had only gone two feet.

Behind me, Burst had dragged Hank away from Fiskel; they both lay struggling in a tangle of crutches in the hallway. Fiskel was set to push off. Sunder had strapped the rifle to his back, stepped onto the back of the snowshoes, and placed his arms around Fiskel's waist. Fiskel and Sunder shoved off. It was only a matter of four giant steps, and this little game would be over.

The telephone rang. I reached up for it.

"Hello," I panted.

"Hey dude," came a woman's voice. "This is Tammy from New Orleans. Your fan club, remember?"

"Hey babe," I said. "I'm kind of busy right now. How's the fan club doing?"

"It's just Marcia and me for the moment. James went hitching around the country to get his head together. That's not what I called about."

"Can you make it short?" I said. I looked over my shoulder. Hank leaped onto Sunder's back. Burst made a wild grab at Hank's ankles, and hung on. Though Fiskel was tilting backwards slightly, the four of them were making inexorable progress across the surface of the rug.

"Well," she said, "*Perfect World* is getting kind of *nightmarish*, isn't it? When you gonna go to a club or something? This is supposed to be a Perfect world, pal. Take us to the sock hop of the gods, my Ian!"

"Trust me, babe," I said. "The day's not over yet. Gotta run."

"Wish you could," she said.

I hung up the phone and dived for the bed. I rolled over twice and landed on my feet in front of Door Number Two. No handle. And I'd left the remote-control unit in the bathroom. I was scratching at the door with my fingernails, shouting, "Wake up! Wake up!" when strong clumsy hands took hold of me, and I found myself held fast, a prisoner.

captured

"Open the window, Mr. Burst," said Fiskel Yahr.

"Good idea," said Hank. "Let's get some air in here. We got a lot to talk about. I can messenger contracts over here, I can set up Ruthie on a conference call, we can clear this whole thing up right now."

"It won't open," said Burst. "It's one of those climate-control deals. Plexiglass," he said, pounding on it. "Nothing's gonna open this baby. This is one solid baby."

Fiskel frowned at me. I was wrapped in bedsheets like a mummy, and they'd stuffed the remote-control unit in my mouth.

"Take his feet," he told Sunder. Fiskel grabbed my head, and they threw me against the window. I could feel the window yield as I bounced back onto the lavender couch.

"Ng," I said.

Hank was nodding his head up and down. "That's the ticket," he said. "Make the technology work *for* you."

"Hit him, Mr. Sunder," said Fiskel.

Sunder hit Hank on the arm as hard as he could.

"I accept that," said Hank, his face ashen. "That's acceptable."

"You," said Fiskel to me, "are going to tell us where the Destiny Commander is."

"Gar?" I asked.

"Or," he said, "my greasy men, my dirty workers who grease the wheels, are going to keep throwing you at that window until you, or it, breaks. Pick him up."

Sunder reached for me. Thinking fast, I depressed one of the remote-control buttons with my tongue. The silk curtains slithered shut behind Sunder. Burst panicked at the sudden noise, and fired the rifle at the window. The curtains stopped in their tracks, and collapsed with a dying whisper. A round bullet hole was revealed in the window. Sunder shook his finger at me.

"Fight fair," he said. "Give me a hand, Mr. Burst."

Favoring his leg, Burst grabbed my shoulders, and Sunder my legs. They were well into their backswing, and my head was facing the door. The door flew open, and there, in the hallway, backlit by the soft fluorescent light, in black leather, with a trademark sneer curling his lip, and a blue-black curl of hair nudging his pale forehead, stood Elvis. He was wearing skis, and he pushed into the room, heading straight for us as fast as a bullet.

Burst and Sunder dropped me. Sunder went for the rifle, but Elvis was too fast. He sailed over the lavender couch, leaping out of the skis. The skis speared into the window and stuck there with a quiver. Elvis did a somersault in midair, stiffening his fingers in mid-flip. He landed nimbly on his feet, on the back of the couch, and karate-chopped Burst and Sunder simultaneously. They fell senseless to the ground. Elvis turned for Fiskel Yahr, but he was already sliding away on his snowshoes and was halfway across the room.

"I'll see you in Moscow, Mr. Shoales," he shouted over his shoulder, then he was out the door, and the door slammed shut behind him.

"Ruthie," Hank, oblivious, was saying into the telephone. "Is that you? Operator?"

"I'm sorry I'm late, sir," said Elvis. "I just now collected my messages." He removed the remote-control unit from my mouth.

"Where did you learn to ski like that?" I asked.

"I made a little thing called *Colorado Blue Ski Party*," he said. "A Universal Picture, 1964, with Miss Jill St. John and William Demarest. Once you pick it up you never lose the knack, really. We've got to get you out of here, sir."

"How?"

"Through the window," he said. He strode over to the window. "Huh!" he said, and punched it in the middle. It fell into smooth pebbles around him, and black clouds swirled into the room. The moon was a blank face in the sky.

"You gotta know where to hit them things," he said with his quirky trademark grin.

"Operator?" said Hank. "I'm trying to reach Moscow, North Dakota. It's a new listing. Ruth? Ruth, is that you?"

"Gimme that thang, man," said Elvis. He snatched the receiver from Hank and held it to my ear.

A woman's voice struggled through the distance and static. "Hank," it said. "I fired you three months ago, you've got to stop calling me."

"Ruth?" I said.

"Who is this?' she asked.

"This is Ian," I said. "Ian Shoales."

"So?" she asked.

"So I'm coming for you, baby, across space and time and the weight of the dead years, across the span of experience and bad judgment and mistakes too close to call, through politics and bad weather, and suffering and danger, I'm flying to your sweet arms *tonight.* I don't know how, but look for me, darling, I'll be in your eyes tonight."

"Great," she said. "Bring a cheeseburger, will you, the food here's terrible."

I heard the dial tone. She'd hung up on me. I like that in a woman. I'd have mixed feelings about any woman who didn't have mixed feelings about me. I didn't have mixed feelings! Amazing.

Elvis had picked up Hank with one hand and thrown him into the hallway. Burst and Sunder followed. Elvis turned to me. He thrust his hip to one side, cocked his left leg in, like a half-knock-kneed man, and pointed his finger at me.

He said:

elvis speaks

Sir, I'm just a hick who hopped the gypsy train of fame. Where I growed up, the South done never rose at all. Folks was poor and folks was hurtin'. The colored people hid their hearts, and the white folks envied what they could not see. Sir, as a child I hid under the black man's porch in an attempt to emulate that sweet soul thing. How was I to know, sir, that my heartfelt copy would take over the real? That was never my intention. I *had* no intentions, sir. My life was a fluke. It was an unchaperoned party, and things got out of hand.

Once I was under the porch with the hammer of strings and the work-boot taps on the boards, and that boxcar pound and that gospel sound, and the next thing, sir, my roots were uprooted, and what I did ain't what I done, and what I done ain't what I did no more. I thought I had it all, the fire and the sky and the reasons why, but it all turned to dust in my hand, sir. It all turned to dust in my hand.

a brief pause while elvis gets a drink of water, and ian (annoyed because he is still trussed up on the lavender couch like a babe in swaddling clothes) takes advantage of the brief pause to grasp the

*remote-control unit with his teeth so he can see what's happening
on the tube while elvis tells it like it is*

like it is

Sir, as you move down this highway of sorrows,
you may wish for a fine Cadillac car—and I have had many fine
Cadillac cars—and you can sing sweet surrender with your body-
guards, and you can pop them pills and watch the scarves drift in
the flash from the fans who adore you.

You can have the world, and all the millions in it, and your
houses and your mansions with your billiards and your greens, but
sir—it don't mean nothing. It don't mean a thing. You got to have
the love of a fine, fine woman, sir, to fill that empty house inside,
it takes the love of a fine fine woman to fill up that emptiness within.

a friendly reminder to elvis concerning the reality of the situation

"That's just great, El, but I'm still trussed up
here, and there's nothing on TV but these damn game shows. If I'm
gonna rescue a maiden and save the world, hadn't I better get a
move on?"

"Sir," said Elvis, undoing my bonds, "I have a gift for you."

I restored circulation through a grudging use of isometrics, as
Elvis unfurled a Giorgio Armani suit. It was a little wrinkled (he'd
been carrying it in his backpack), but it gleamed still, as pale blue
threads caught the indirect hotel room light.

I slipped it on, and knotted the gray silk tie on my tapered gray cotton shirt. I was still wearing my battered Street-huggers™ and there were some nameless stains on them, but there are only so many concessions I'll make to fashion, and two aching feet are not two of them.

"Sir," said Elvis, "if you'll stop watching television for a moment, I have something else that will aid your journey."

He held a ticket envelope in his outstretched hand. I took it from him. Inside was a one-way ticket to Moscow, North Dakota, on Convergence Airlines. I was flying coach though, the cheap hick.

I turned off the set. The channels kept spinning. I turned my back on it.

drive he said

——————————— Elvis had fashioned a makeshift parachute from the monogrammed sheets on the bed. I took a firm grip, a deep breath, and perched myself on the windowsill, my airline ticket clenched between my teeth.

"Good luck, sir," said Elvis. He spun around, and kicked in the face of the television. "And don't get distracted from the call of your heart, y'hear?"

"Yeah yeah yeah," I said between clenched teeth. Elvis gave me a little push, and I was airborne, through the window, and falling, drifting like a scarf Elvis would throw to the front row, dropping like an unwelcome memo from upstairs, floating on the bad breezes, swooping like the amputated wing of a scorched angel. I fell, I tried to fly, I aimed my wobbling self at the circle of besieged limos. I hoped, not for the best, but for the least of the worst.

A slight current bore me slightly up, and my flannel wings carried me to the very center of the money-laden vehicles. I smashed through the protective shell of briefcases, hit the pavement, and rolled, just like Jeff Chandler (*Sky Divers*, 1954). I checked my suit for rips as Sarge gripped my hand and grinned. From beyond our little circle, the roar of those in want was deafening. And my breach in the briefcase defense would be all they needed to pour in.

I took the ticket from my mouth.

"Pack up the billions!" I shouted above the din. I made a circle in the air above my head with my forefinger. "Let's roll 'em."

I leaped into the back of Sarge's limo, a spacious stretch Huff, and we peeled out. The interior of the car was filled with bouncing Vuittons. Grabbing an armful I strapped them in with seat belts and looked anxiously out the window.

Our car was swarming with beggars. Sarge made a handbrake turn that spilled a panhandler into the street. A tight U-turn with a fishtail sent three independent producers sprawling, the pages of screenplays flying in the air.

On our hood was a grim-faced auto-parts salesman whose obvious determination to cling to his samples case made his fall inevitable. "Just five minutes," he yelled hoarsely. "Just five minutes of your time!"

On my left I saw a swarthy man in the garb of a convict. He was clinging to the door handle with the cruel gleaming hook he had for a hand.

"Hey," I yelled, rolling down the window, "you're supposed to be in lover's lane scaring the heavy petters. Get outta here."

"Sorry," he shouted, letting go.

Our next sharp right took care of the auto-parts salesman. That left only a guy on the roof. I poked my head through the open window and looked up there. It was Randee! He was riding the roof of the car like a surfboard, and in his hand he clutched the Destiny Commander.

"Boy am I glad to see you," he said. "Take this thing back, man. I'm seein' things on teevee that shouldn't be there. Psycho Boy's got a kid's show and his own brand of breakfast cereal. That ain't right. My dog Feedback is doing stupid pet tricks on David Letterman, man. My dog's been dead for two years, and David Letterman ain't even *on* yet. I'm tellin' ya, there's something wrong with this picture."

He tossed it to me, and I caught it.

"Hey Des," I said.

"Why Mr. Shoales," said Destiny Commander. "What a pleasant surprise."

Sarge made a sharp left and Randee went flying.

"I'll just get off here!" he screamed.

We'd been making circles in the lot; now the long line of limos had shaken their parasites and we headed for the exit. Our limos laid patches and squealed out of there. The wisps of our great friction spun up and vanished like a breath in winter air, and we hit La Brea, heading south.

"LAX," I said. "Step on it. I've got a flight at eight."

"No problem," he said.

Two trucks veered out of our way and smashed into each other meaninglessly, just like those dumb car crashes on the otherwise excellent "Rockford Files." Our sixty limos got into a tight formation, and beyond them, behind us, a cluster of headlights, the reflected eyes of beasts of prey, hit La Brea, and started to gain. The roar of their acceleration was the roar of a starved lion. This fool and his money was the prey.

future perfect

And there we go, my money, my Destiny, and I, down the exhausted avenues, exceeding the speed limits, on our fast way down mean streets, on our way to that smooth stretch of tarmac, where a big steel bird waits to carry me and my billions away.

If this was a movie we could use the helicopter, *Time Chopper Twelve* (if we weren't already using the chopper to monitor my thoughts as I lie dreaming dreams of me, here in the future, in the Perfect World of Wax, looking back on this dream of my past), but I only have one. Who would have thought simple consciousness would be so complicated?

So there, below us, in a space the size of four football fields, I have constructed, in HO scale, the path of my flight from L.A. A simple switch of the remote-controlled Destiny Commander (stand back of the rail there, kids, that's right), and you can see the City of Angels blink into life.

Ooooooh.

Over a trillion light-emitting diodes were used to create this miniature metroplex. Over seven thousand miles of slots for the tiny slot cars were carefully laid down between the minuscule fast foods and snug bungalows of the greater Los Angeles area. Follow the laser pin-spot, folks, and you can see our little cluster of limos there. Here's the path we took: south to La Brea, then west on the Santa Monica Freeway to the San Diego Freeway, then off on Sepulveda to LAX. Yes, sir, you have a question?

Why didn't you get off in Santa Monica and take Lincoln over? A lot faster than the freeways that time of day.

What I do is get off at La Cienega—

Gentlemen, please!

I push Play on Destiny Commander and you can see there, in the southwest corner of the complex, the lights of LAX, where jet planes, like mutant dragonflies the size of eagles, circle and land, circle and fly away.

Overhead—

Aaaaaaahh!

—the winking wingtips of planes and above them, the night sky, pricks in a black blanket of night, a remote-controlled leak from powerful lamps hung on steel girders, installed by burly bored workmen at great personal expense. Pretty though.

And there—follow the pin-spot—there is my car in the lead, the big stretch Huff, coated with Kelvin T-20, the lightweight bulletproof shielding developed for swift Israeli tanks and since marketed in the U.S.A. as limo protection, and (oddly enough) as a lining for sports coats worn by ghetto doctors, Mideast and South American diplomats, and night managers of 24-hour convenience stores. Incidentally, over one hundred thousand convenience stores were painstakingly handcrafted and reproduced here in the Perfect World of Wax, complete with video games, microwave burritos, and, yes, even unhappy Saudi cashiers, Palestinian cashiers, even a handful of chubby female cashiers from the Valley, their hair moussed and teased in the front, long in the back and sides in a pale teenage parody of Linda Evans on "Dynasty," every strand, every curl etched by hand by hardworking Cambodians and Vietnamese who know the value of survival, but not the value of their own labor—yet.

The silver chain of limos scoots along the worn grooves of the HO slots, at seventy miles per hour (relative speed) down the middle of La Brea. Don't crowd. There's room for all of you. Matter of fact, let's lower the huge Zeitgeist lens (designed and built by unemployed NASA engineers) to bring this action into sharp focus.

There I am in the back seat of the Huff, clutching a briefcase full of money. Almost every car in Los Angeles is on our tail. There's the '57 Panic packed with teens in felony shoes, and there's the two Drove station wagons, filled with small screaming children and haggard mothers. Behind the Droves, tiny Hurry after Hurry, full of divorced men on the lookout for a fast buck. There's the writers in their swift Dazes. And there's the constellation of RVs and souped-up Circles. Thousands are converging. And what do they want? They want what I want. Money and revenge.

There's a Fury bristling with firearms! See! Every person in every house is taking to the streets. The Japanese models spin out of control. Look, in the empty houses, the televisions, too, spin out of control. The airwaves are jammed with the signals of dreamers. Advertisers have nothing to sell. The networks go down in flames. Consumers can't handle the hideous variety.

And everybody knows that I'm to blame. Everybody knows whose hand pushed the buttons.

There's Burst and Sunder in a big black Kessler. There's the rocket launcher poking from the passenger's side. Kaboom! Missed!

Wow!

We veer around the pothole (easily fixed, a simple illusion, really). The La Brea tarpits are far behind us now (amber and ink, packed with plastic dinosaurs from Toys R Us; it's the only place we skimped, folks, hope you're not disappointed at the lack of dinosaurs in this world). Burst and Sunder switch their Kessler into overdrive! But they miscalculated, switched too soon, they zoom past our caravan (see the little round surprised O's of their mouths? Nice touch, I think), and overshoot the on-ramp, which we hit doing eighty. We smash through the homemade roadblocks, and head on west.

Applause.

Okay boys. Cool 'er down for a minute. Questions? Yes sir. *How much a thing like this set you back?*

Ninety trillion dollars.

Ooooooh.

Yes ma'am?

Wouldn't that money have been better spent on social programs?

I'm a social critic, lady, not a bureaucrat. Like what social programs?

Endangered species. The environment.

Oh, a wax museum *isn't* an endangered species? There's one on every block in your hometown, is there?

I didn't mean that—

Get out!

Applause.

Next question.

What's your power source?

Solar power, running water, and windmills. Yes sir?

Can we get on with the show? We gotta drive to L.A. yet tonight.

Let 'er rip boys! Yes, ladies and gentleman, this is the closest thing to adventure this white boy ever had. There's thousands of cars behind us, honking. You can hear the screams of the needy, and even from this distance and scale it's deafening.

What?

Imagine me, in the back of the Huff, flat on my back, my hands over my ears, going "laylerlaylerlayler" at the top of my lungs, Sarge doing the same thing, driving with his feet (what a masterful driver!). We smash through the blockade of angry Teamsters, who want a piece of this somehow. Unions! Management! The pie gets smaller and mouths get bigger! What do we do? The trucks go up in flames!

Oooooooh.

With the tiniest effort of will, without even will, with just one simple push of a button on the patented Destiny Commander, we, like the ancient gods, create reality! What would it *take* for this to be real?

Is this a contest?

No ma'am.

It'd have to be bigger.

But isn't size relative?

Get on with it.

Right! Spectacle! You tourists have no patience! Okay! Down

405! Ka*boom*, okay? The PLO rocket launcher misses the motorcade, hits the insurance building.

Aaaaaaah!

Down it goes, imploding. We go through Yugos like snowplows through snowbanks. And we signal right! Off the off-ramp, south down Sepulveda, there's the screech of brakes behind us, a massive pileup!

And ahead, ladies and gentlemen, the big Convergence 666 revs its mighty engines on the runway. Four men in blue suits climb furtively aboard.

Excuse me Mr. Shoales, but isn't that guy with the binoculars—?

Speak up, son, don't be afraid.

Well, wasn't he the federal agent pretending to be the clerk at L'Hotel Ennui?

Good eye, kid. Good memory. You didn't have to peek at page 101 to jog your memory?

No sir. It's not like this is a Russian novel or anything.

Yes, ladies and gentlemen, four feds are on my flight, we'll see why next chapter, but *there!* At the end of the runway, Burst and Sunder, looking efficient at last, set up their rocket launcher, and wait.

Back to the action! There's a money-seeker with bald tires! A screech of brakes and he goes down, smoking! Isn't this amazing?

Kind of!

These toys used to be for the rich, but in a book, my friends, in a dream, in *America*, the poorest of the poor can share jollies with the wealthy. Mechanical devices! Spectacle! Waterworks! Figures in wax! Look, these are our *lives* down there. We drive! We watch TV! We explain ourselves constantly to ourselves, because we can't remember who we are anymore. We just don't know anymore. We don't know who we are.

I have to go to the bathroom!

Look! We hit the tarmac! I spill out of the car! The plane is waiting! Say it!

Go Ian go!

And there's the sleek massive silver 666 and its great steel sides yawn open. "Faster," I'm yelling. "Faster."

Faster!

And there's Burst and Sunder lobbing in missiles. The explosions walk in closer, the swift footsteps of an angry god.

Faster!

The burly workmen heave my billions in. The bombs step closer, and closer and closer, and I'm ushered aboard by the indifferent flight attendant, and there we taxi, and there we roll, and there—

Lift-off! Oooooh!

And there are the black bursts of flak in the sky, and the cars of our pursuers do wheelies in front of our plane in a vain attempt to stop our lift-off. A bomb goes off close by. It jars the luggage door, and it opens as we tilt to starboard, trying to remain airborne, and there's my nine billion dollars, little tiny briefcases, no bigger than the heads of nails, falling out of the plane and through the air. They hit the runway and they crack open, a marvel in workmanship. The little tiny notes, like tiny twinkling green stars in the night sky, sprinkle and flutter, and scatter like leaves before a winter wind, and then the people are upon them.

Bye-bye money.

Bye-bye.

And the Kessler pushes its way through the pressing crowd, and soon they're all lost behind me in the distance. Bye-bye.

Bye-bye.

This way out, ladies and gentlemen. Watch your step.

your top ten countdown
top ten epochs of the western world

1. **Prehistory** Discovery of fire, wheel. Underestimated epoch.

2. **Mediterranean Empires** Tragedy, comedy, and torture introduced as public entertainment. As people have more things to remember, writing things down becomes more important. Leisure invented, and, subsequently, slavery. Invention of the thought *What will people think of me when I'm dead?* We know too much about the Greeks and Romans.

3. **Middle Ages/Renaissance** Christianity battles the old gods,

wins. Merchants arise. Science makes lists. The imperial ships set sail.

4. ***Enlightenment*** Reason battles Christianity. Only the meek lose. The blood runs in the streets of Paris. The third world created, but not called that.

5. ***Victorian Age*** Darwin, Freud, and Marx. Introspection meets the world. Christianity settles into its easy chair to listen to soothing music. Art gets sappy. Sex gets regulated.

6. ***Roaring Twenties*** The Western world gets drunk, falls down. Henry Ford stays sober and shapes the way the future will operate. Anonymous thugs consolidate control in the Soviet Union and Germany. Photographs! Motion pictures! Radio! Machine guns! Flying machines! Physics as art.

7. ***World War II*** This was the Big One, and it's still being fought forty years later. Only now are we beginning to absorb its effects. No person on this planet was unaffected. Such a statement was not possible before World War II.

8. ***The Fifties*** In Africa, revolution. In Central America, revolution. In the Caribbean, revolution. In South America, revolution. The Soviets turn countries into satellites to make scabs for their raw flanks. The U.S., unthinking in its terror of the wounded Russian giant, begins its dopey and cruel foreign policy. The Third World becomes the pawn in a stupid struggle between baffled giants. Europe wiped out as historical player. The sitcom. Rhythm and blues. Elvis. Hungary. Guatemala. The Shah. Afternoon movies starring Gene Autry on local television. Suez. Childhood. Insomnia.

9. ***The Sixties*** Vietnam. Bay of Pigs. U.S. takes center stage and flounders around. Our allies grumble and back away. Mick Jagger gets rich. Muddy Waters doesn't. Half-understood Eastern religions become briefly popular. The thugs of the Soviet Union grow older. The death of narrative, except in genre fiction. Slow-motion in movies. The demise of CinemaScope, boo hoo. Silly psychedelic music. Drugs. Science becomes religion. Man on the moon. Headlines

replace wonder. Experts replace thinkers. Youth replaces wisdom. Death of the attention span. Ian Shoales graduates from high school.

10. ***The Eighties*** The decline of disco. Advertising logos attain mythic stature: Coke vs. Pepsi. Nothing means anything. Christianity becomes a joke: Christ wants you to be rich! The world hates the U.S. but loves its culture. *Dallas* was all a dream! Might use that idea in a book sometime. Elvis becomes a saint. Michael Jackson gets stranger. Death of Bob Marley reverberates. Video. Computers. *Rambo* for God's sake. *Rambo* Reagan for God's sake. Photo opportunity replaces foreign policy. Death throes of the Cold War. Global Village on fire. Something's got to happen. Digital recording. Satellite dishes. Cable. Every old dream goes up in smoke, and in the ashes, yuppies arise, tiny white insignificant greed-heads with no redeeming social value. AIDS. Trivial Pursuit. *Perfect World*. Dream on.

the miracle of flight

When the lights of Los Angeles had disappeared to nothing, I pulled my gaze from the window and looked around. The flight attendant, safely locked in her seat, gazed at me coolly.

"Is there a movie on this flight?" I asked.

"The question is irrelevant," she said. "You won't be with us long enough to see a movie."

"How about free drinks?" I asked. "Those little airplane peanut bags, something like that?"

"Nothing is free, Passenger Shoales," she said. "Everything has a price."

As if that were a cue, and maybe it was, four men in blue suits emerged from the bathroom. One of them was the clerk from L'Hotel Ennui, still wearing his binoculars.

"I'm Ted," he said. "I won't shake hands, no time. Just tell me, how'd you know?"

"Know what?" I asked.

"Know what," snickered the blue suit on his left, dryly.

"Know that ProCorGenTel was a front," said Ted.

"I didn't," I said. "Front for what?"

"Front for what," snickered the blue suit on his right.

"Should we tell him?" said the blue suit in the rear.

"Why tell him what he already knows?" said the blue suit on Ted's left. "A waste of energy."

"Why don't you tell me what you think I know," I said. "And then I'll tell you everything I know that you don't know I know."

"Guy makes sense," said blue suit in the rear.

"We're Peripheral Intelligence Agents," said Ted.

"I *thought* you were PIA," I lied.

"They call us the Sandblowers on the Beltway," said the suit on Ted's left. "We blow sand in everybody's eyes."

"Signal left, turn right, that type of thing," said the suit on the right.

"We use ProCorGenTel to launder money," said Ted.

"ProCorGenTel almost made the Fortune 500 last year," said the suit in the rear. "Pretty good for a company that doesn't make anything."

"Except Destiny Commander," I said.

"That's just a McGuffin," said Ted. "A lure. The Soviets are developing a jamming device. We wanted them to think we've got the same thing only smaller."

"Theirs is about the size of a Shetland pony," said the suit on the right. "You know the Soviets."

"We kept trying to get the Soviets to bite, but they wouldn't bite," said the suit on the left.

"That's when you stepped into the picture," said Ted. "They sent their best man. Dmitri, master of disguise."

"That wasn't Fiskel Yahr?" I asked.

"Oh you're good," chuckled Ted. "I almost believe you don't know."

"You ever tried telling the truth?" I asked.

"Only if we're sure nobody will believe it," said Ted. "Been a long long time since we said what we meant, right, boys?"

The boys nodded, then shook their heads.

"What if I were to tell you that Destiny Commander is real?" I asked. "That it really works?"

"He's good," said suit in the rear, admiringly.

"Who do you work for?" said Ted. "Come on."

"Freelance," I said.

"That's why we've never heard of you," said suit on the right.

"America's falling apart," I said. "It's been overwhelmed by the force of its own dreams."

"Listen," said Ted. "If we do go down, then they're *bound* to go with us. There's nothing so seductive as chaos. Especially in covert operations."

"So what's your plan?" asked the suit in the rear.

"I'm gonna meet a girl," I said.

"Right," said the suit on the left.

"A girl," said the suit on the right, winking. "Good cover."

"Watch out for Dmitri, son," said Ted. "It's all a big game in Moscow, North Dakota. Don't let that game get real."

"We'll see you at the Circus," said suit in the rear. "Midnight."

"Don't do anything stupid," said suit on the left.

"Or you could find your ass in a world of hurt," said suit on the right.

"We'll be in touch," said Ted.

They marched to the exit, opened it, and jumped out.

"Hey," I said to the flight attendant. "They jumped out."

"They chose to jump, and now you must make that choice," she said. She removed a small pistol from her apron. "Please proceed in an orderly fashion to the exit nearest you."

"Can I take the headphones?"

"Do whatever is necessary and take what you desire, but leave now or I'll be forced to shoot you. The choice is yours."

I took the headphones, walked to the door, and jumped.

"Wait a minute!" I shouted back at the plane. "I don't have a parachute."

"There's a five-second margin for error," her Dopplered voice came back. "You should make your connection if the plane is on schedule."

The night air was brisk as I fell. I wished I'd brought a jacket, or even a blanket from the plane. Oh well. It would be a brief fall, one way or another. I'd either make my connection or a greasy hole in the ground. Either way I had time to kill. I threw the headphones away. I hate music on airplanes. They only have music to disguise the roar of flight.

So I fell on in silence. I pulled Destiny Commander from my pocket.

"How powerful are you, pal?" I asked.

"Powerful," it said. "But fragile."

I pointed Destiny at the night sky and turned it on.

The stars blurred in the sky, and fuzzy images took shape.

11 MOVIE—

Made for TV. 2 hrs. "Portrait of a Meter Maid" (1979) Lindsay Wagner.

"Well," I said. "Looks like things are getting back to normal."

"Normal?" said Destiny. "Bad movies spread across the western hemisphere?"

"Reception's not too good," I admitted.

"I've been handled too much today," it whined. "I need new batteries."

NIK HAWAII FIVE-O—

McGarrett gets a crewcut.

Maybe Destiny had a point. Television programming spread across the night sky appealed to me personally—after all, stars aren't visible in a city anyway, and I'm a city boy now—but there were disadvantages. Sure, the programming was free, and no set was required, but programming was random, and who do you call if the picture goes on the blink? And the implications were disturbing.

Did this mean the universe itself was a cable subscriber? If it was, then if you *weren't* a cable subscriber and you lived in the universe, did you exist?

(RANDEE) NOISES YOU
CAN MAKE
WITH YOUR
MOUTH—

Variety

Suddenly the solution to this problem seemed so *easy*. Why hadn't I thought of it before? I took Destiny Commander and threw it away from me as hard as I could.

"Wait," said Destiny, falling.

"What do you mean, wait?"

"You don't know the code!"

"What code?" I shouted.

"The code to save the world," came its dwindling voice.

"I don't want to save the world," I said. "I want to meet my girl."

There was silence. Wind.

(SHOALES) MOVIE—

Action/Adventure. 4 hrs. "Chain
of Fools" (1988) Stunning aerial
photography and stuntwork
highlight this tongue-in-cheek
spoof of spy thrillers. Pamela
Reed, Debra Winger, Chrissie
Hynde, Miss Manners, Ian Sho—

The image blinked off. Destiny must have hit the ground. The blurred stars came back into focus. Below me, through drifting clouds, I could make out the bright lights of a city on the prairie below.

On my right, seemingly from nowhere, a prop plane zoomed into view. The doors of its side flew open, and strong burly hands grabbed me. The wind of my falling suddenly ceased to roar in my ears. I was suddenly warm, aboard my connection. I was warm, safe, and on my way.

Yes, forces I didn't understand had thrown me out of an airplane, but—they had grabbed me before I hit the ground. In a sense, then, I guess you could say The System works.

promotional brochure for moscow, north dakota

In the final days of the Cold War, we made bombs so we would not use them. We shot certain people so others would trust us. We betrayed those who trusted us to gain the trust of others we did not trust. Eventually we couldn't trust anybody, so we avoided those areas where trust was necessary.

This made life easier in some ways, harder in others.

The Family, for example, suffered. (The Family maintained a tenuous existence at the whim of advertisers, who nurtured the image of the family in order to sell those things which families needed.)

Romance, on the other hand, flourished. Romance was perfect for the Cold War. Romance does not engender love; it engenders attraction. Romance is based on jokes and beautiful lies. Like Romance, the Cold War used both jokes and lies in service of a larger objective: self-perpetuation. When the ground on which we stand is based on lies, the lies must be intricate enough to seem true, or at least real, or we're standing on nothing.

And so it was with the Cold War: lies were revealed, more lies told, until foundations were as thin as thin ice. Everything disintegrated, and we fell through into the darkness. We knew we had to fall. Everything must fall. That is the way of the world.

In the final days of the Cold War, the sophisticated network of weapons grew and the diversity of human society dwindled. People became willfully ignorant. They just did not want to learn anymore. There was too much to learn, and yet it was required of them to learn it all. Oppressed by the weight of what they could never know or possess, the poor drank hard, took drugs, and had children.

The poor were considered a problem by the rich. The rich dressed well again, in the final days of the Cold War. They affected top hats and tails, sumptuous gowns. The bohemians of society, artists and actors, danced with the rich, the old stately dances. The rich went everywhere by horse and balloon. They hired the poor to drive them and to protect them from the other poor. Some of the very rich transformed entire cities into cities from another era. They placed guards (again the poor) at the border with orders to kill anyone who arrived without an invitation. The black market on forged invitations thrived, and punishments for forgery were severe.

The rich held no hopes at all. Their desire was for an earlier time, when their wealth meant something, when wealth was an end unto itself. If they could have, they would have transformed the entire world into an earlier time. But it wasn't cost-effective. The laws of nature stood in their way.

In the final days of the Cold War, we forgot how the weapons worked, and where we had them hidden. We entertained certain fantasies about what our enemies were thinking, but neglected to watch what they were actually doing. We attached so much importance to what might happen next, we forgot to pay attention to what was happening at the moment, and to what had gone before. And, when things didn't turn out as we had dreamed, we called it betrayal. That's when we brought in the police and secret agents. That's when the killings began. That was the end of the Cold War.

And that is when, in hope and fear, Moscow, North Dakota, was created. Conceived at a summit meeting between the two formidable world powers, it was conceptualized by a special team of Western theme park designers and Eastern circus impresarios. It was built by a special architectural team, who for security's sake were not told the names of the others on the team.

Funds for Moscow, North Dakota, were raised through arms

sales. We sold arms to our enemy's allies, and they sold arms to ours. The entire transaction was strictly supervised by clandestine specialists of both powers.

The day-to-day running of Moscow, North Dakota, has been achieved by a joint effort between the internal security forces of both powers, and Marriott's Food Host. Many colorful booths provide a wide variety of foods from both cultures. And the hundreds of exhibits and rides testify to the hope implicit in this place. The hope is to create an entertaining home for fear, and to make terror fun once more.

If you enjoy Moscow, North Dakota, please tell your friends. And look for a Moscow near you very soon.

last leg

We were descending. The official flight attendant for Glasnost Airlines, Olga, slipped a leg beneath her to occupy the seat on the aisle next to me. A sensible square-toed shoe dangled from her foot. A ladder of runs ran from her heel to her calf, disappearing under the hem of her regulation-length gray skirt. She was silent as I peered at her with my peripheral vision. She was too friendly. Even for a flight attendant. She was crowding me. She could have been a spy.

"We will land soon," she said in her unaccented English. She reached under the seat and removed a bottle of vodka. In Moscow there are no caps on the bottles. You strip the foil and drink till the bottle's done.

Together we drained the liter, even though I hate vodka. She threw it against the heavy door of the cockpit, as was the custom. She smoked a cigarette, dropping the heavy cork filter onto the dirty floor of the airplane, where they joined countless others. I was her only passenger.

I sat overlooking the wing. My window's thick green surface had three deep scratches, dark and dirty on the edges, as if these marks had been carved long ago. I was reminded of the portholes in the forehead of the Statue of Liberty. I remembered when I saw the Temple of Dendur at the Metropolitan Museum of Art; I was struck by how this temple, separated from its natural environment and history, in the context of vast gray skyscrapers and commerce, seemed *just tiny*. In the context of New York City, the Temple of Dendur seemed new, and small. And the Statue of Liberty had to feel the weight of years before it gained stature as a symbol, and then it too was displaced by the weight of commerce, and became another logo. The propeller spun as slowly as the blades of a ceiling fan.

"You are wondering," mused Olga, "how many traitors have been hurled from this great height."

It wasn't a question. It certainly wasn't a statement of fact. I decided she was just filling the empty space with her voice. I said nothing.

As we circled for clearance, mist obscured the city. I could see lights under that cold fog, like headlights underwater. I imagined I had a camera in my head, sending important data back to square-jawed men in blue suits, huddled around monitors in a stainless steel room. I felt safe, mobile. The sky around us was filled with planes and helicopters, all bringing people into Moscow: tourists, spies, diplomats, lovers.

As we lowered, the mists parted, and I could see the long rows of parked tanks, the rows of hopeful emigrants (all hired by the Tourist Bureau) as they snaked out across the frozen wastes, their torches bright and held high.

"In Moscow," said Olga, "the air is always crisp. Moscow is like no other city."

The stone walls of the mini-Kremlin squatted on the horizon. Thin patches of snow revealed expanses of frozen black earth between the airport and those gray walls.

The airport itself gave the illusion that it had been painted green fifty years before, and not touched since. As I deplaned, a heavyset man with a dark fringe of beard knelt before me, clasping my knees and sobbing. The people beyond the barbed wire applauded. Beside me, Olga snapped her fingers and burly security officers hauled the man away. My suspicions of her were confirmed. I followed her, therefore, as she walked briskly away from me.

I found myself at the luggage carousel, though I had no luggage. I watched the suitcases flow by. The noise of the conveyor belt was deafening. I looked around me cautiously. Olga had disappeared. I was alone.

The origin of the flow of luggage was a dark jagged hole halfway up the wall. As I watched, a sweating man in a red shirt appeared in the center of the hole, bracing himself as he stood. Pieces of plaster crumpled under his weight to fall on the conveyor belt in silent white explosions.

"To whom does all this luggage belong!" he shouted in anguish.

I looked around me, and saw a large man with silver teeth. He was standing at a right angle to my body, grinning, his eyes focused on some point in the middle distance. His eyes darted over to me, but his head did not move.

"Is any of this luggage yours?" he asked.

I shook my head.

A large walkie-talkie dangled from his belt. His gray suit was too large for him, and the weight of the walkie-talkie pulled his trousers below his hips, revealing the faded flowers of his underwear. He hitched himself up with a swift motion of his stubby hands.

"Welcome to Moscow," he yelled. "I will take you to your hotel."

at the gates

The yellow brick road leading to the entrance to Moscow was lined with souvenir stands (I'M A LITTLE MUSCOVITE t-shirts, postcards of spires), metal machine-gun bunkers, and guard booths disguised as Fotomats. A few hundred yards before the gates, two tall white men wearing earphones noted our passage with a brief nod, and waved ahead to bald men in winter jackets, who cradled submachine guns (like infants) in their arms.

We came to a halt in front of the rusted iron grating. A voice addressed us from a loudspeaker.

"Why have you come to Moscow?" said the voice.

"You're a tourist," whispered my guide.

"I'm here to meet a girl," I said.

"*Tourist,*" hissed my guide.

"Are you sure you're not a tourist," said the voice. "Are you sure you haven't come to see the sights?"

I gave up. "Okay. I'm a tourist."

"Enjoy your stay in Moscow," said the voice. "Please remember, all documents traded must be reported to the Disinformation Committee. Have a nice day."

A bright flash went off in my face. I knew my startled face was reappearing behind closed doors, wired to D.C., faxed to Russia, filed and forgotten until such time as my behavior raised a silent alarm. Then the image of my startled face would be pulled, and the secret police would strap on their guns and come for me. That was all part of the fun.

Blinking away the spots before my eyes, I gazed at the big stone entrance to Moscow. On either side of the archway, a huge granite bear and marble eagle clasped talon to paw in a frozen gesture of friendship. Bear and eagle stood on the shoulders of two burly stone gents, with granite sleeves rolled crisply up, as they grasped the beasts on their shoulders with sinewy veined forearms bulging. *Now* that's *art,* I thought.

The iron grate slid open with a clatter and we moved forward. My silver-toothed guide, who was clinging to the outside of the taxi, began shouting hoarsely. His voice was muffled by the pane of Thermal-Gard between us.

"Taxicabs were first introduced to Soviet society by a Western defector. Here in Moscow, North Dakota, the cabs provide a unique riding experience. Only one person can fit in each cab. Therefore a seat inside the cab is considered an honor and a privilege. Other passengers are obliged to cling to the outside of the vehicle."

He leaned into the curve as we rounded the Nuspeke Centr, looking at me ferociously, his teeth chattering. Around me I could see trams decorated with the official logo of Moscow, North Dakota: the Fuzzy Bear Hugging the Winking Eagle. Each tram carried upwards of fifty tourists who snapped pictures furtively and giggled, while the smiling driver shook his head and chuckled into the public-address system: "Now folks, you know pictures are forbidden here."

"How do I rate this special treatment?" I asked. "How come I'm not riding the tram with the package tours?"

"You said you are a tourist," he said. "That means you are a spy. That means we must keep a special eye on you."

"I'm not a spy," I said. "I'm just another American, Jack, looking for a good time. How about this place, Monroe's Doctrine? I heard it's a nice club. I heard that American singer Ruth D. is playing there tonight."

"There are no nightclubs in Moscow," he said.

"There aren't?" I asked.

"Of course there are, but I am not permitted—" He looked at the back of the driver's head meaningfully, tried to shrug and almost lost his grip. "Facts!" he shouted. "Traffic accidents are rare and the drivers very friendly!"

Our driver waved at us grimly.

"Most deaths in Moscow," continued my guide, "are attributed to anxiety, exposure, and alcohol abuse. You know, natural causes. Ah, here is your hotel!"

As I got out of the cab, he handed me a small engraved card which contained only the name LUCILLE. I was told to commit this name to memory, then he took the card away from me, placed it in an aperture on the side of his walkie-talkie. The card was sucked in with a hiss, and a small conduit of smoke rose from the antenna. He hitched up his trousers, saluted me, and took my seat inside the cab.

"I'll be watching you," he shouted, as the cab took him away.

l'hotel ennui

"Welcome to Moscow, sir," said the desk clerk. "Will you be buying or selling?"

"Buying or selling what?" I asked.

She laughed. "Secrets," she said. "You must be a first-time visitor."

"I dunno," I said. "Both, I guess." She bore a remarkable resemblance to the woman in the Time/Life commercial. "Say," I said, "aren't you Judy? From the typing pool at ProCorGenTel?"

"Oh hi, Mr. Shoales," she said. "I didn't think you remembered me. I got transferred here this afternoon. So you want the Double-Agent Package?"

"Your judgment."

"You have some messages," she said.

"Yeah?" I said. "Read them to me."

"Let's see," she said. She shuffled pieces of paper. " 'If you wish to regain your lost billions, bring the Destiny Commander to the Circus at midnight,' signed 'A Friend.' "

"Okay," I said.

"Um. 'Give it to me or you're a dead man.' Signed 'F.Y.' He wouldn't leave his name."

"Got it," I said. "I know who it is."

" 'Where's my cheeseburger? Ruth.' " Ahhh. 'Watch your step. You're being watched. Ted the Fed.' And this one— 'I'll swap you the plans for the Laser Blast Ikon Smasher for your plans to the Microwave Brain Thief.' No signature."

"What?" I asked.

"Oh, wait a minute, I'm sorry. That's another room."

She placed it in one of the mail slots behind her. A gloved hand on the other side removed it as she turned back to me, smiling.

"Very well, Mr. Shoales," she said. "A diplomatic courier will bring the complete Espionage Vacation Package to your room. Your rooms *are* bugged, of course, part of the complete service we provide. Remember to intuit the rules and obey them before they change, and you should have a very enjoyable stay."

"Thanks," I said, taking the key. "Oh, by the way, I'm looking for a nightclub."

"There are thousands of nightclubs in Moscow," she said.

"Monroe's Doctrine?" I asked.

Her smile vanished. "That's restricted information. Front!"

A bellboy bearing a striking resemblance to the actor Joe Don Baker appeared from nowhere, grabbed me around the waist with one hand and ran me up the stairs to my room. He hurled me into a corner.

"No tips!" he shouted, and stalked off.

My hotel room had no door. This is very common in Moscow hotels. Everybody knows this. Still, I pretended to be shocked and surprised; there was no need for whoever might be observing me to know what I knew. I got up and dusted myself off.

The telephone rang. I picked it up.

"Sorry to hear about your loss," came a familiar-sounding voice. "But did you ever think that you're in possession of something even more valuable? Worth trillions?"

"And how many limos is that?" I asked.

"I'll make contact at the club tonight," said the voice.

"Where is the club?" I asked, but the line was dead. I lay down on the bed. I closed my eyes, but kept my thoughts discreet. I hoped to fall into a brief dreamless sleep, like any old hand at espionage, but thoughts of Ruth entered unbidden. The old monks and old spies are probably right: if we could conquer our own desires, a Perfect World could be ours. But how can you desire a desireless world?

I opened my eyes again, swung out of bed, and padded across the threadbare rug to the window. Below me on the street the police were bunched together under a streetlight, singing a mournful song.

I heard a growl behind me. I turned in time to see a wolf come through the open door, followed by, of all people, my poolside folksinger, Lucille. She looked healthier. She'd gained some weight since last night. She wore a miniskirt and spiked heels.

"Don't mind the dog," she said.

"That's a wolf," I said.

"I said *Forget the dog*," she said. She gave the wolf an angry look. "You sit." The wolf just stood there, its pink tongue lolling and bobbing from the side of its mouth. "You got any menthol cigarettes?"

I shook my head.

"That's the only thing I miss," she said. "And cats. They got a law against cats here, who knows why, they don't have rhyme or reason for nothing here." She looked at the wolf. "See? See how you done me? I don't have nothing 'cause of you!"

"Why are you here?" I asked.

"I'm here to show you the sights," she said. "I'm supposed to make you feel at home."

"I mean," I said, "are you a Marxist?"

"No," she said. "I just got fed up with L.A. You want to see Lenin under glass? That's always open. They just put Kennedy in there too. They got 'em sitting up together in golden chairs, with the smiley bears and eagles dancing all around. It's something to see."

"I came to meet a woman," I said.

"No women here," she said. "See the leaders under glass. Then go home."

"Where's Monroe's Doctrine, Lucille?" I asked.

"I—" she started. Her lower lip was quivering.

"Don't say another word!" It was Hank's voice, Hank from Murray & Murray. He rushed into the room. "Not to this impostor. Fiskel Yahr, huh? Don't listen to him, honey, he's got nothin', he's a nobody." He rubbed her neck with one hand while jabbing at me with the other. She half-closed her eyes and looked away.

"I never said I was Fiskel Yahr," I said.

"Fiskel's coming tonight," he said. "With the entire management team. We got the chairman from the Central Committee, we got Bernie from Discord Music. And you know what? They're coming to see Lucille, man, not your precious Ruth. Lucille's gonna blow Ruth off the stage, man. We don't need you there with your Ruth this and your Ruth that, there's only room for one female singer/songwriter in the album-oriented rock scene, and who is that gonna be?"

"Me," Lucille said feebly, her eyes closed.

"I can't hear you!"

"Me!" shouted Lucille. "Me!"

Suddenly a rift appeared in the hotel wall and quickly widened. Two men, wearing bags on their heads, appeared in a blur. One grabbed the wolf and one grabbed Hank, and they ran back into the wall, which closed just as swiftly behind them. I was struck dumb. Lucille just slumped and sighed.

"They took your wolf," I said, regaining my voice.

"Thank God for small favors," she said. "Be something else

next time most likely. They always saddle you with something, wooves and duties and what have you. This here's better'n L.A. but it sure ain't good."

"And what about Hank?" I asked.

"Isn't he sweet? He just called me up, out of the blue, and here I am."

"They took him too," I reminded her.

"They always taking somebody," she said.

"Listen," I said. "If I get your wolf back, will you trust me? Will you help me find Ruth?"

"What do you want me to trust you for?" she said. "I don't want the damn dog."

She was either lying or telling the truth. If she was lying I could believe her or not. If she was telling the truth I could accept it or not. It was that simple.

"You have something for me," I said.

"Oh yeah," she said. "Here."

She dug into her purse and tossed me a manila envelope.

"That there's your Vacation Package," she said.

"Thanks," I said.

"What you want to thank me for?" she said. "I do what I'm told."

I felt the need for action. I ran out the door at a sprint, to what destination I really had no idea.

vacation package

————————— Here's everything you need: forged papers, a small blue automatic, a list of contacts.

Here's your scenario: certain people believe you are in possession of a top secret device. Whether or not you possess this device is irrelevant. It only matters what people think.

Here is the list of your pursuers: United States federal employees, Soviet government employees, the park police, a certain master-spy named Dmitri, whose intentions are unclear, and an unknown madman, whose identity you must discover, who means to use the device you may or may not have to destroy the world as we know it. Stop him if you can! The adventure will culminate at midnight at the Circus, where you will learn the truth about Moscow. And yourself!

Enclosed you will find black-market maps of the Moscow Underground. Once underground you must find your archenemies. You will be tortured briefly. After this confrontation please proceed to the Hall of Former Lovers, where you will meet "Susan." "Susan" was your lover in college. You joined ROTC; she joined the Weather Underground. You haven't seen each other since 1971. Whether she will help you or betray you remains to be seen.

Selected memories: the night you and "Susan" made love in the rain, protected from the damp by the dark dry archway in the quad. The night you quarreled. The separation. The abortion. Fill in the details. Use your imagination!

Things to remember: "Susan" is not real, but she could have been. Avoid the nightclubs. You enter the nightclubs at your own risk. The park police cannot help you in the clubs. There are places, even in Moscow, the cops won't go. Good luck. And watch your back. For your convenience you will be photographed every step of the way on your adventure. To obtain your handsome leatherette souvenir espionage memorial album, please have your Visa or MasterCard ready as you exit the park.

These top secrets will self-destruct in five sec—

the game is afoot

"Ow," I said, "Jesus," dropping the smoking package. It curled to nothing at my feet. I sucked my fingers and checked the maps. Yes, there was the telephone kiosk, with the old-fashioned rotary dial. I dialed "W-A-K-E-U-P," the code I'd been given, the trapdoor creaked open at my feet, and I went down the wobbling circular staircase.

The tunnels below the city were stainless steel, clean, modern, and bright. I knew that here lay the hidden life of the city. My papers were in order: false, as they were supposed to be. I was armed. I held paper secrets to trade, if I needed to trade. And I knew that this kind of behavior, skulking around forbidden zones, was expected of me. It was why Americans were so welcome in Moscow. Every bureaucrat I passed in those bright tunnels was wreathed in smiles. I pulled my gun and stopped one of them.

"What am I looking for?" I demanded. I hoped I was speaking in code.

He gestured vaguely, toward what could have been any of three corridors. In disgust I let him go, and stepped through a door at random. I found myself in darkness as the door slammed shut behind me. A spotlight hit my eyes, and I backed into the door.

"And how do you like Moscow so far?" asked a smooth voice beyond the lights. I shrugged, blinking.

"Do you miss American ways?" said the voice.

I stopped shrugging, not wanting to indicate nervousness. I knew that this interrogation was only a matter of form. Questions are asked daily. They put gels on the spotlights so visitor's eyes will not be irritated. A hand from the shadows handed me a pair of polarized sunglasses, and pulled a chair out for me. A dark fizzing liquid, without ice, appeared at a little table by the chair. I sat, let the liquid sit, and waited.

"You Americans," said the voice, bored. "You can be whatever you want to be, but you only want to be what you imagine others want you to be."

"And what do you want me to be?" I asked.

"Cooperative," he said. "You may as well cooperate. Americans make terrible spies."

"I'm not a spy," I said.

"You see," said the voice. "You are telling the truth. I'll tell you a lie to show you how it's done. You are wasting your time here."

"Am I?"

"Of course not. I was lying."

"Were you?"

"Enough!" came a second voice. "You have to be careful with

this one." Whether the voice was speaking for my benefit or not, was hard to tell. "Don't demand so much from him. Just remain silent. Sooner or later, Mr. Shoales will tell you everything. You love to talk, don't you, Mr. Shoales?"

"I'll tell you nothing," I said.

"Don't underestimate yourself," said the second voice. "You don't know what you'd do."

True enough. Suddenly I lunged forward and slapped the spotlight with my hand, reversing the beam and revealing, in its glare, the owner of the first voice, Fiskel Yahr. I leaped forward and grabbed his beard. His rubber head came off in my hand, revealing a leathery brown bald head, with two glittering black eyes behind wire-rim glasses. *Dmitri,* I thought, remembering the Vacation Package, *the master of disguise.*

The owner of the second voice retreated in the shadows before I could make out his face. Strong burly hands grabbed me and sat me back down. The spotlight went out, and there was silence.

In Moscow, it is considered polite to respond to every question. I sat patiently, waiting for another question. I waited through another five minutes of silence, then slipped away.

I headed for the Hall of Former Lovers, where "Susan" lived. All contacts live in official dormitories, so everybody can keep an eye on them. It is mandated by Congress and the Central Committee that every fifth contact must be a double agent, and every third of those five a triple agent. Every sixth triple agent must be an agent of a minor power, selected at random by the Swiss delegation. Despite the maelstrom of regulated betrayal, however, the contacts' view of Moscow life was unspoiled. They are allowed to be students well into their forties, if they wish. They are allowed to write intense poetry. They are allowed to adhere to certain beliefs which they may or may not passionately hold, but which they may express (within the guidelines, of course). They may hold masked balls in the cafeteria. They are tolerated by the authorities.

The only propaganda on this "campus" is the loudspeaker, the bulletin board, and the occasional poster tacked to the wall. Among friends and in the classroom, there is no propaganda. All the professors, however, are spies, either KGB or CIA. It's hard to tell. Nobody really cares anymore.

I stepped up to the kiosk that marked the entrance to the Hall of Former Lovers.

"State your business," said a flat American voice. *Definitely KGB*, I thought. *Nobody's that bland.*

"You're wrong about that," said the voice. "Your business."

Panicked by this feat of mind-reading, I thought of a still mountain lake surrounded by a brick wall. This is the protective image most recommended by the brochures. I said, "I wish to visit 'Susan.' "

The bar lifted. I trudged through gray snow. My breath rose in clouds, and the sounds of Moscow rushed in the distance: singing, wheels on cobblestone, a mighty hum and rumble beneath my feet. The ground shook gently.

Ahead of me in the middle of the quadrangle, the five-sided beacon of the Capitol Dome blazed perpetually. It is said that this beacon, the so-called "Czar of the West," will burn as long as men wear chains—Or was that as long as men *forged* chains? Or *thought* about chains? Or mentioned chains in passing—? I made a mental note to recheck the brochure.

I approached the door and knocked. I disguised my voice and my name and hoped I was fooling somebody.

"It's you," she said, opening the door.

"That's a tautology," I said. I put a finger to my lips and showed her my gun (part of the Package).

"What are you doing with that?" she whispered. "You know it's forbidden."

"It's a Bic," I said. "Harmless."

I fired a shot at the wall. The capsule exploded with a dull thud. Thick streaks of red ink clotted the wall.

"Susan" sighed and turned away from me. I imagined I could remember her walk. She reminded me of Girlfriend Number Four. That SloMo walk, that serious demeanor. She had been easily offended, I remembered, and I, of course, was easily offensive. It just wasn't meant to be.

She opened a dusty book and sat down on an ottoman, curling her long legs beneath her. She was my age at least: late thirties; she looked good: tight blue jeans and t-shirt, no bra, of course. Not only were bras considered politically incorrect when I was in college, they were, and are, an indispensable absence in most works of popular fiction, whose authors seem to think that a reader's attention needs to be captured and recaptured by constant reminders that women do indeed have breasts. Well, she had them. She was barefoot, and her long hair was clean and uncombed. The ottoman was the only visible piece of furniture in the room.

I strolled to the window in the uncomfortable silence and watched the turgid Missouri River move south. Distant washerwomen on the banks pounded overcoats with rocks. *Nice touch*, I thought. *Lends a bit of verisimilitude.*

The silence dragged on. Girlfriend Number Four had had a scar on her knee, I remembered, where she'd fallen at age six on a broken bottle. Had I traced that scar with my lips? Maybe. Maybe not. I'd traced *something* with my lips. I was out of practice. *I must check the scenario, the brochure, my memories.* I shook my head to clear it.

"Why is everybody here?" I asked. "Where is the magic of Moscow? Who believes it? Who's against it? Why did I lose you to the Cold War?"

"You're outside the guidelines there," she said, not taking her eyes off the book. "Those questions aren't in the scenario."

"Maybe we have different scenarios," I said.

"Let's see," she said, looking up at me at last. Her eyes were an intense blue in the glare of the single bulb. "I planted a bomb at the ROTC center at school. It didn't go off. It just lay there and fizzled, then took off like a dud firecracker, through the window. It left a shower of sparks, and sheared off two branches from that old oak tree in the plaza, remember?—and came to rest in a lilac bush. The bomb had my prints all over it. Not only was I the laughingstock of the campus, I'd committed a federal offense. I took it on the lam and ended up here. You? You went to 'Nam as a first lieutenant and got fragged by your own company before a week had passed. Now you walk with a limp and tell every girl you meet you got it in a firefight. You work as a file clerk in the State Department but you allow girls to think you're some kind of spy. You stand by the fireplace at parties, rubbing your leg and giving bitter little smiles. I spend my days here, reading historical romances, and now the tortured path of history has brought us here to this bittersweet moment. Can we live down the past? Can we fan the old flames? What do *you* think?"

"I don't know," I said. I was impressed by her contempt. I walked around the room some more. I tried out a limp, but it didn't feel right, so I dropped it. "You might be a double agent. You might not be my enemy at all."

"*You* might be a double agent," she said. "And if I were a triple agent, where would that leave us?"

I tried to figure out where we would be left, but it made my head hurt, and I gave up.

"Let's keep it simple," I said. "I don't know if I'm supposed to remember you, and *if* I remember you, what my feelings are supposed to be. I don't know if your bitterness is directed at me, or some other guy who left you burning. Maybe you're just an actress with a bitter mask, maybe you're Mata Hari, or another *Big Chill* fool who can't let go of youth. You could be a pistol in the sack, no strings on the pleasure, or you might be a gal with emotional price-tags on every caress. Maybe you're a shell that cracks with kindness, or an iceberg that melts, I don't care. What did or didn't happen was a thousand years ago, and this is now, and I'm looking for my baby, and I'm wading through the crowd, will you help me or not?"

"I always used to hate it when you got on jags like that," she said. She pointed at the window. Something about the gesture, the wide flakes of snow in the dark beyond the window, made me remember a movie I'd seen in college, a silent Soviet film. The Cossacks on their big white horses, riding into the heart of a disturbance. The mob like a wave of flesh. The escape across the tundra, the pursuit by wolves. The aristocrats, Michael and Tatiana, standing calmly in their white furs, listening to chamber music, as the hot fires creep closer to the Palace. Packing the weapons in wooden crates. Stolen kisses in a shattered ballroom, a painted moon glimpsed briefly through a jagged hole in the ceiling. Was this an illusion created by a Soviet-style low-frequency radio wave? Was this a flashback to those chemical dreams we shared those sweaty nights so long ago? Was it merely a memory?

The lights had come up. I saw her face before me.

"There," she said. I looked where she pointed. "The big wide doors with nothing on them. Knock three times. The password is *Perfect World*. Just say *Perfect World* to make them take you in." She

lowered her voice to a whisper. "Come to the Circus, midnight.
Come with her, if you find her, or come alone."

"How will I know you?" I asked.

"I'll be the one who looks like me," she said. "And you'll be
that fabulous guy I remember so well. The boy without the joy. The
man with such a way with words."

"Hey," I said. "I just say what I think."

"So do insects," she said. "They just have tiny thoughts, that's
all."

She shut her book with a bang. Dust danced in the harsh light.

I let myself out. I went past the Destruction of Public Buildings
Building. I took pictures of the door before me with my digital
minicam. There was no need to do this, but it was expected of me.
It was part of the Package.

from the brochure

What do we know?

Well, we know that marriages are a help on the income
taxes. We know that sex only occurs when partners are
drunk. We know that people here are sentimental about
Lenin and Kennedy. Their remains are preserved, like figures in a wax museum, in the Square. This Muscovian
sentimentality, however, has more to do with political ne-
cessity than nostalgia. Any great city needs dead leaders.
We must have faces on our coins. We must have statues.
We must have museums deeded by the dead. We must have
parkways named for civic leaders, and streets named for
heroes from our past. These are the traps of history, and if
we try to free ourselves from those traps, we face the danger
of living in a city with no names at all. If we face the truth—
that Lenin was a ruthless butcher, and Kennedy a spoiled
philandering fool—we are left with empty squares. We are
left with gaping holes where the statues used to be. We are

left with a wounded civic pride, and grief at betrayal. That is the price of demythologizing our history.

What else do we know?

We know that conversation in Moscow is always guarded, always interesting. The river is cold, black, and sluggish, like a reptile from a childhood nightmare. We know that the tundra borders the city (Astroturf, actually, sprayed daily with water, which freezes in seconds, making unofficial escape officially impossible). Beyond the tundra, beyond that icy plain, the bonfires of the barbarians are a thin circle of fire in the distance. Beyond that, the arroyos and buttes, where the coyotes roam and howl, and sidewinders sleep away the long winters. The color here is like the color of colorized movies: one appreciates the effort, but wonders if it was worth it.

There are long lines for vodka and prescription drugs. Only one apartment in five has a lightbulb, and one in those five conceals a microphone. Attractive women disguise their bodies in lumpy clothing. Only the elite get cable. Sunlight is rare. Shadows grow in the maze of buildings. One person in seven has a scar. Everybody has a secret. If you don't have a secret you will never get in. If you don't have a secret, you will never be allowed to leave.

The most important thing to know: when they laugh in Moscow, they are laughing at your freedom.

nobody's sweetheart

——————————— "Perfect World," I whispered after my knocks, and the doors swung open. A blast of heat assaulted me.

My silver-toothed guide stood in the doorway. He had changed into a Hawaiian shirt and was carrying a tall frosted glass with a little umbrella sticking out of it. "I am drinking a zombie!" he said. "Par *tee!* Come on in before you get shot, just kidding, haw haw!"

He pounded me on the back and hauled me into the place.

"What time is it?" I asked.

"Don't ask!" he said. "Moscow is like Vegas! There are no clocks on the walls! Bogey!"

Bogey the bartender turned. He was a short, basset-faced man wearing a burnt-orange vest over his Hawaiian shirt.

"A zombie for my American friend!"

"No drinks," I said. "I need something to eat. You got cheeseburgers?"

He shook his head. "Piroshki," he said.

I shook my head. "Egg salad on wheat?" I said.

He shook his head. "Moldavian veal pie," he said.

I shook my head. "Patty melt?" I asked.

He shook his head. "Black bread from the Ukraine," he said.

"You got a menu?" I asked.

He shook his head.

"Gimme the bread," I said.

Bogey turned from me abruptly, as though I was an argument he'd given up hope of winning.

"Ah my friend," said my guide. "Tonight when we dance the *Krezbach* we will touch the ceiling!"

"That's something to look forward to," I said. I scanned the room for signs of Ruth. The room was a concrete box that had been painted pink and green in a hopeless attempt to suggest some kind of "Miami Vice" ambience. The stage was a platform held together with duct tape, and scattered among the half-empty tables were a dozen or so dead palm trees.

"Ian!" came a voice. "Oh Ian! Hi!"

I looked over. There was Judy sitting at a table with—of all people—R.J., Lucille's ex from Tennessee. His head was down, his lower lip quivering, and his hands were clenched together in front of him.

"Excuse me a minute, Ivan," I said to my guide.

"Vladimir, you kidder!" He slapped me on the back so hard it sent me trotting past their table and into the wall. I pushed away and staggered over to Judy.

"Did you bring him?" I whispered to Judy, hanging on to a palm tree while I caught my breath, indicating the depressed R.J. with spasmodic nods of my head.

"Well," she said primly, "it's a long story. Right after you got fired this morning, a bunch of us went after you to take you out to lunch. I couldn't find you, but I ran into the street person named Randee."

"Two E's, like the river," I said.

"I kept trying to give him a dollar," said Judy, "so he could buy a string for his poor guitar, but he kept running away from me. Finally he pointed this little black thing at me, and the next thing I knew I was on some kind of TV game show, where I won a round trip for two to Moscow, North Dakota. Of course they explained to me that I'd just be a minor character in your book, but what the hey, I figured—it's free. Not only that, when I got back to the office, I found out that I'd been transferred here. So I could move here for nothing, and take somebody with me! So I was racking my brains thinking who could I bring, when I found R.J. sitting on a curb weeping, and I thought, *What an amazing thing! Kismet has sent this man to me!* I said, 'You come with me right now and we'll take your mind off whatever your problem is.' "

"Lucille," said R.J.

"Right! And you know what? She's singing here tonight!"

"She doesn't want to see me," said R.J.

"That's what I call serendipity," said Judy. "Just like Sting."

"That's synchronicity," I said.

R.J. lifted his head and saw me. His eyes squinted shut.

"You're that Murray," he said.

"No," I said. "I'm that Shoales."

It was too late. He'd leaped across the table, sending margaritas flying, and had me by the throat.

Judy said, "You know each other too! Is *that* synchronicity?"

"Get him off of me," I croaked.

"Now boys," said Judy. "I don't know if Moscow's ready for all this male energy."

I was starting to black out. Out of the corner of my dimming vision I saw limping Burst and quick Sunder. They grabbed R.J. and pulled him off me.

"He took my baby from me!" screamed R.J.

"I'm so glad he's coming out of his shell," said Judy.

Sunder was busy dragging R.J. away. I clutched my throat.

"Mr. Yahr would like to see you," said Burst. "Hey, it's *really* Mr. Yahr this time. I'm sorry about all the trouble we caused you. See, we thought that guy who wasn't Mr. Yahr *was* Mr. Yahr but then it turned out he wasn't. Mr. Yahr."

I saw Fiskel in a corner of the club talking on a cellular phone, and totting up figures on a pocket calculator.

Burst and I limped over to him, past Sunder, who was knocking R.J.'s head onto a tabletop.

"Stop that rough-housing, you two!" said Judy behind me. *"Men."*

"Zombies!" I heard Vladimir shout. "When you drink them the moon rises!"

I was about to sit down with Fiskel when Hank slid into my seat.

"Fiskel?" he asked. "Hank. Murray & Murray. We met in L.A. Have a nice flight? It's great to see you here. You're gonna *love* Lucille. She's been on 'Saturday Night Special,' she's been on 'Boppin',' she's done a 'Rock Comfort,' all in syndication you understand, over seven cities nationwide, but we have hopes, we have hopes, and we hope you're a part of those hopes."

"Who is this person?" Fiskel asked me.

"Hank." I coughed. "Murray & Murray."

"Right," said Hank. "Hank. Murray & Murray. Let me tell you a little story about the music business, long as we're all here, about disco and Jesus. I had Ruthie signed, man. I mean we were in the studio. So what happens? Disco takes a dive, and Marty—Marty Goldensohn, head of A & R—gets so depressed he checks into a cheap motel to kill himself, opens the Gideon Bible, and boom! Isaiah 5:12. *And the harp, and the viol, the taboret, and pipe, and wine are in their feasts: but they regard not the work of the Lord, neither consider the operation of His hands.* These words lace into his heart, one week later, okay? *One week.* He will only produce music with musical instruments mentioned in the Bible. *You* see drum machines in there? Twenty-four track? I sure as hell don't. He's calling all over town trying to find taborets and sackbuts, groups are hocking their glitter, and me and Ruthie are in the toilet again. So."

He wolfed down his white wine and jerked his head at the stage.

171

"So that's the kind of talent Ruthie is," he said. "The kind a religious man won't touch. Think about it. Now Lucille now, *she's* got talent. Ruthie had talent, don't get me wrong, ask anybody. She wasn't trouble to me, she was a *challenge* to me, she was artistic, you know, she had integrity. She had the integrity, I had the business sense. We were a helluva team. The interface between art and business is a very interesting area. Course she's kind of *old* now, thirty-five if she's a day, she's not young and vital like Lucille. Energy. That's what interests me. And I'm sure, Mr. Fiskel, energy is what interests you."

"Uh huh," said Fiskel. He nodded.

Sunder hit Hank on the arm as hard as he could.

"I accept that," said Hank, turning white. "Hey, it's been *great* talking with you again. Enjoy the set. Lucille I mean, not Ruth. *Please*, oh God. I love you! Gotta run."

He was up, and I was down.

"Pay no attention to that creep," I said. "You should really watch Ruth."

"Look," said Fiskel. "I can't enjoy myself. I can't. I'm a wealthy man. I've had some fun with you, sure, but fun's fun, and money's money, and you have something of mine, and I want it."

Sunder said, "We'll waltz around with you some more if you want."

I said, "I *am* considering some other offers."

"Well, consider this," said Fiskel. "It's mine. It's not yours. I inherited Destiny Commander when I bought the company. You stole it from me."

"Here's my question about that," I said. "When Wilkie gave the company to me, that made the dingus mine. How can you take something that was given to me by somebody else? Doesn't that make you sort of an Indian giver once-removed?"

"Uh huh," said Fiskel. "Well, you dance around with your thoughts, Ian, but if you don't give that thing to me you will find yourself in a lot of trouble."

"You will find yourself in the hospital," said Burst.

"If that thing is not here on this table in front of me by the time I decide to leave—and I could decide to leave any minute now—you will be in as much trouble as I can command, do you understand me?"

"All right," I said. "I don't have it here. I have to messenger for it."

"You have until this Lucille, whatever her name is, finishes her set."

"Aren't you gonna stay for Ruth?"

"No, I am not. I have to be in Boston by six A.M."

Vladimir approached me. "No talk," he said. "Drink."

"Excuse me," I said. I walked away from Fiskel's table. Ted the Fed fell in step beside me, tagged by his federal fellows. They were all wearing Hawaiian shirts under their blue suits.

"Got my eye on you," said Ted cheerfully. "You know there are laws against trading with the enemy?"

"Yeah?" I said. "Who's the enemy?"

"That's me, dear boy," came a smooth voice. I turned to see bald-headed Dmitri.

"Dmitri!" shouted Vladimir. "Come drink with me!"

"Business first," said Dmitri.

"Can I tag along?" said Ted the Fed. "As a tourist?"

"By all means. Here. Let us take this dark booth, so our body language will not reveal our true intentions."

"Make your pitch, Dmitri," said Ted.

dmitri's pitch

"You Westerners are so fond of mythology. Here in Moscow we have no need for mythology. Your Romeo and Juliet, for example. This is a tragedy which would never have occurred in Moscow. If a competent doctor had been with Juliet, her self-destruction need never have happened. Here, in Moscow, we can kill a dog and bring it back to life! We can tap your thoughts with microwaves. We can microwave your thoughts with wiretaps. What equivalent miracles can you present?"

"In America," I said, "you can hover like a vulture around foreclosure auctions, then make a million giving seminars telling others how to do the same."

"But did you know," said Dmitri, "that capitalism is the leading cause of diabetes in millionaires? Hmm?"

"Tell me," Ted said to Dmitri, "do you have documentation of these phenomena that they would accept in Geneva?"

"Facts," snorted Dmitri. "Moscow is merely a legal fiction, like Disneyland. Like the United States, and the Soviet Union. We only exist through consensus. I am fond of facts, but a true fact is rare. I would rather express my opinions. Would you care to hear one?"

"I'm not a journalist," said Ted. "I'm a tourist."

"Ah, you are a spy. You are here to follow the secrets. Well, I will tell you a secret: the missiles are perfect now. There's nothing more to be done. Now that the missiles are perfect, we can finally put them away, and move on to something else. Right, Mr. Shoales?" He winked at me.

"Right," I said. "Sure. I have what you want."

Everybody thought I had what they wanted. It was only a matter of time before I was found out. And I had the sneaking feeling that if these people found out I didn't have Destiny Commander, I would be killed. At the very least I'd have to pay for my hotel room.

"What will you give me for it?" I asked.

Olga, my flight attendant/spy, appeared at Dmitri's side.

"Do you wish me to seduce him to find out what he knows?" she asked him.

"No," said Dmitri. He turned to me. I was nodding furiously. He said, "What you have is so priceless it is worthless. I will give you your life for it. I will wait here in this booth for your answer until the young woman has finished her set."

"This conversation is just fascinating for a tourist such as myself," said Ted. "I don't work for the feds, by the way. That's a misconception."

"Do you wish me to seduce *him* to find out what he knows?" asked Olga.

"That would be great!" said Ted.

"No," said Dmitri.

"Does this mean you aren't going to stay through Ruth's set?" I asked.

"This discussion is terminated," said Dmitri.

Ted grabbed my arm and pulled me away.

Conseils d'entretien

1. Remettre la cassette dans sa boîte en plastique après usage.
2. Ne pas toucher la bande afin d'éviter éraflures ou pertes de son.
3. S'assurer que la bande est bien enroulée, la resserrer au besoin en faisant tourner légèrement l'une des bobines.
4. Nettoyer le cabestan, le rouleau entraîneur et la tête d'enregistrement à la fréquence spécifiée par le fabricant.
5. Éviter les expositions à la chaleur excessive, à l'humidité, à la lumière du soleil directe et aux champs magnétiques intenses.
6. Protégez ses enregistrements préférés en retirant les pattes anti-effacement du bord supérieur de la cassette.

Tips für Gebrauch und Lagerung

1. Cassette immer in der Plastikbox aufbewahren.
2. Das Band nicht mit den Fingern berühren.
3. Vor dem Gebrauch sicherstellen, daß das Band fest aufgewickelt ist. Lockeres Band durch Drehen einer der Naben anspannen.
4. Tonwelle, Andruckrolle und Aufnahmekopf Ihres Recorders regelmäßig nach Angabe des Herstellers reinigen.
5. Folgende Bedingungen bei der Lagerung der Cassetten vermeiden: hohe Temperatur, Feuchtigkeit, direktes Sonnenlicht und starke Magnetfelder.
6. Versehentliches Löschen bzw. Überspielen wird vermieden durch Ausbrechen der Aufnahmesperren am oberen Cassettenrand.

Sugerencias para su manejo y almacenaje

1. Mantenga el cassette dentro de su cajita protectora, cuando no se use.
2. No toque la cinta con los dedos, puede sufrir arañazos o caída de señal.
3. Asegúrese de que la cinta esté enrollada en el carrete del cassette, sin juego perceptible. Antes de su reproducción tensione la cinta girando con suavidad uno de los rodillos.
4. Limpie el eje impulsor, el rodillo de pinza y la cabeza grabadora en los intervalos especificados por el fabricante.
5. Evite exponer los cassettes al calor excesivo, la humedad, la luz directa del sol y a los campos magnéticos intensos.
6. Preserve sus grabaciones valiosas quitando las lengüetas para evitar el borrado, ubicadas en el borde superior de su cassette.

FULL LIFETIME WARRANTY

If, at any time during the life of this audio cassette, it is found to be defective, 3M will replace the cassette free of charge, provided the audio cassette has not been damaged through misuse or handling. Such replacement shall be 3M's only responsibility or obligation. For replacement, send the defective audio cassette postage prepaid to 3M.

GARANTIE TOTALE

3M s'engage à remplacer, à tout moment, toute cassette défectueuse retournée par l'acheteur à ses frais, à condition que cette défectuosité ne provienne pas d'un usage anormal ou d'une erreur d'utilisation.

eagle flies on friday

"Payday," whispered Ted in my ear. "You're young, but you're good. You've got 'em all lining up at the window. The entrepreneur on a string and the Commie on the hook." He turned to his fellow men in blue. "He promised the thingie to both of 'em." He chuckled and turned to me. "They'll kill you, you know. I love it."

"What if I don't have this thing?" I asked.

"Oh that's a hot one," he said.

His three pals chuckled darkly.

"Then *we'd* have to kill you," said Ted.

"I thought you thought it wasn't real," I said.

"We lied," said Ted. "Damn. You caught us again."

"We must be slipping," said his pals, in unison.

"There's a third party involved here," said Ted. "And you just might be the hook we need to net that big fish. Go to the Circus, son, at midnight. Sit with the gypsies. We'll be there, in disguise. Don't worry. We're behind you. Every step of the way."

They beamed at me and walked away, fooling nobody.

The place was starting to fill up. A group of Republican women sat at a table together, glancing around suspiciously and clutching their purses.

"You're Ian Shoales, aren't you?" came a voice to my left.

Ruth? I wondered, turning to find not Ruth, but a young woman with pink hair and an orange jersey. She was carrying a mauve notebook and wore a button which said DIE DANCING!

"Yeah," I said.

"I'm Michelle," she said. "I write for *Falling Sky*. Hank invited me. The premiere issue will be out on the stands next month. If I can break a few unknowns like Lucille for them I'll be in a good position. I'm freelance now, but they're looking for writers. You should submit something."

"I'll never submit," I said.

"Ha ha," she said. "Isn't this place *wonderful*? Have you checked out the bartender?"

"You mean Bogey?" I asked.

"Bogey," she giggled. "He's wonderful. This whole place is so *Soviet*. And isn't Lucille too much?"

"Not yet," I said.

"It's like she's not a folksinger," she said. "It's like she's *describing* a folksinger. Just like Moscow, North Dakota, is a *description* of Moscow. And description is a judgment. Wait a minute—"

She wrote down in her notebook *Description is a judgment.*

"I know this sculptor," she said, "who refuses to sculpt anything. He shows other people's sculptures and puts his name under them. He says art is just a history of images, and the true artist either erases history or tries to arrange the images in an interesting pattern. Don't you think that's wonderful?"

Her pencil was poised.

"No," I said.

She laughed, then stopped herself and frowned at me.

"Are you trying to insult me?" she said wonderingly.

"Not very hard," I said.

"Oh," she said. "That's wonderful. That's so *Ian.* I might use it in my lead. I *love* irony!"

The bright video lights suddenly hit the stage. Vladimir stood in their glare, blinking.

"Good evening, ladies and germs," he said. "Haw haw! Welcome to Monroe's Doctrine, a little bit of Latin Quarter here in frozen north. I will be your Soviet presence for the evening!"

"Go go go!" shouted Michelle. "He's so cute," she whispered to me.

"Contras look out!" growled Vladimir. "Texas here we come! Just kidding!"

Hank appeared next to me; he had all the fingernails of his left hand jammed against his teeth.

"How'd you escape anyway?" I asked.

"Huh? From the police? I confessed. Just sign whatever they put in front of you, and they have to let you go. That's the law."

R.J. staggered up to us. I flinched, but he went past me and weakly clutched Hank's throat. The poor guy was running out of strength.

"Murray," he mumbled.

"They retired," croaked Hank. "I'm Hank, Murray & Murray." Hank looked at me. "Is this guy important?" he gasped. "Should I tolerate this?"

I shook my head. I had my own problems.

"For listening pleasure," said Vladimir. "Welcome please the singing sensation, Lucille!"

Lucille took the stage, as the packed place quivered with applause. Damn. They loved her and she hadn't even sung anything yet. I had to convince a top Soviet spy, a maverick capitalist, and a team of federal agents that not only did I have what they wanted, they could have it too. And I had to find the mysterious Big Fish that Ted the Fed had told me about. I broke a chair on R.J.'s head as Lucille began to sing.

"Shh," Hank gasped weakly, as R.J. fell to the floor. And where was Ruth?

pick to click

LUCILLE (SINGS)

Ohhhhh. Ooooooh.
I met him through a cultural exchange program.
I was only seventeen.
He was a Russian border guard.
And I was the homecoming queen of Nashville.

R.J. (SHOUTING HOARSELY)

Lucille!

CRASHING NOISE.

IAN (SHOUTING HOARSELY)

Ruth?

HANK (SHOUTING HOARSELY)

Shh!

LUCILLE (SINGS)

Well, one thing led to another.
And I was arrested as a suspected spy.
I don't know why. I don't know why.
He was assigned to guard me,
Though it was obvious he adored me.
I was arrested! He caressed me.
I was oppressed! But he undressed me.
Friskily frisking me under the sky.
I don't know why. I don't know why.
We have way too many armies!
Let's sing this song out loud!
Mushrooms are for omelets. Not for clouds. Everybody!

sheer perfection

I looked around. Everybody in the place was singing along. Clapping their hands. Weaving back and forth. Lighting their lighters in the air. Lighting matches. Burning their draft cards. Burning their passports. Vladimir was weeping. Sunder and Judy and Burst were doing the Wave. Even Fiskel Yahr was tapping the calculator in time to the music. Michelle stood beside me, scribbling furiously.

"Have you ever seen Ruth before?" I asked her.

"Old hat," she said, scribbling. "Seventies. That's going to be the thrust of my article. The new woman. The same as the old woman, only ironic about it."

Jesus, I thought, walking away. I needed a drink.

I went to the bar. A woman was sitting there with her back to me.

She was shaking her head. "A club sandwich?" she asked.

Bogey shook his head. "Boiled sturgeon," he said.

She shook her head. "Chips?" she asked. "Jell-O?"

He shook his head. "Cabbage roll," he said.

"Where's my black bread?" I asked.

"Coming up, sir," he said.

"And a couple of Norsk Blebs," I said. "That tart Norwegian ale."

She turned around. Her eyes met mine. My eyes met hers. They introduced themselves. Our eyes made eyes at each other. Our eyes touched knees under the table. Our eyes held hands and then let go. Those hands made magic gestures and made the table rise.

"You got the soul of a poet and the eyes of a cop," she said.

"You think so?" I asked.

"I don't know," she said. "A girl's gotta say something."

She touched my face. I got all tingly.

"You have bruised eyes," she said. "I hate that in a man. I hate all men," she murmured.

"I don't blame you, baby," I said.

Her eyes got sleepy. My heart went *boing*. I felt damp and squishy. *Oh mommy help me.*

I said, "I'll pull the fat from the fire, honey, I'll walk the black-cat trail. I'll argue with the cops if you want me to. I'll throw out the first ball and march in the parade. I'll kiss you where you ain't been kissed and I'll bring you a handful of the dark side of the moon."

"I could go for you in a big way," she said.

My hot flashes got the cold sweats. Nerve central turned pink.

"Let's make a baby," I said.

"I'd rather adopt," she said.

"And waste your precious genes?" I said.

"Adopt a new attitude," she said, "I meant."

"My attitude's bad," I admitted.

"I got one of those already," she said.

"I got enough attitude for two," I said.

"Oh hallelujah," she murmured.

She had those lips. A warm pool at dawn. Hers touched mine.

It was one of those kisses, a swim and a nap and a run round the block.

"Take a walk, doc," she whispered. "The way you talk that talk."

Her lips were a fleshy sunrise. I gained a tan all over, and funny muscles moved.

"Your murmurs are shouts from another room," I said. "I don't know what I mean."

"You're losing your wounded look," she said. "You promised me some food, remember?"

"Your black bread, comrade," said Bogey. He dropped a platter from six inches, and the clatter disrupted our little clinch. Oh yi yi yi, if our hours were minutes like the minute just lived, we could all live forever in a flirty paradise. "Your beer," said Bogey.

"Where is it?" asked Burst and Sunder, in unison, still clapping along.

"Where is it?" asked Dmitri, bouncing his bald head to the singalong beat. "Say, this girl has talent. This girl is going places fast!" He inclined his head very slightly at Ruth. "Who is she?"

"Nobody," said Ruth. She smiled. "Just another dreamer making a grab for the ring."

switcheroo

I sighed. "Better make it to go, Bogey," I said. Bogey turned to get foil.

Lucille had finished her song. The applause was thunderous. Everybody in the place was standing.

"Like that song?" said Ruth.

"Not much," I said.

"Me neither," said Ruth. "I wrote it. I wrote it for her as a joke. I never thought she'd use it."

I tried to absorb the shock of her statement. Burst and Sunder stood on one side of me, their hands in their jackets. Olga stood in front of me, and placed her hands in my jacket. Dmitri stood on my other side, placing his hands in Olga's jacket. I slapped his hands away. "Keep it polite," I said. I was trying to think.

"Your black bread, comrade," said Bogey. He laid two small foil packages on the counter.

"He doesn't have it," said Olga, removing her hands from my jacket.

I reached for my bread, but Burst grabbed my wrist.

"One minute, smart guy," he said.

"Pretty clever," said Sunder.

"Aha," said Dmitri.

"Remove your hands, comrade," said Olga.

"Disguising your Destiny as bread," said Burst. Sunder reached for the bread. Olga reached for the bread. They each had a slice.

"Don't be stupid," I said. "Don't open it here."

I nodded my head slightly. Ted and the three feds were avidly applauding with the rest of the audience, but their eyes were on us.

"The Circus," I said. "Midnight."

Olga tossed her slice to Dmitri. Sunder tossed his slice to Burst. Burst and Dmitri backed into the shadows.

"But which one's the Destiny?" asked Sunder.

"I don't know," I said. "But whoever's just got bread, you know what the other's got, and you'll know how to get it."

"What's that supposed to mean?" said Ruth.

"It means I'm hungry," I said. "Say, Bogey—"

Bogey shook his head. "Borscht," he said.

But Olga and Sunder had my arms behind my back and were dragging me backwards off my stool.

"Now you die," murmured Olga. I preferred the murmur of Ruth.

"I'll try to catch your set," I said to Ruth. "Wait for me."

"Till the end of time, lover," said Ruth. She cracked a smile as easy as a cold one on a hot day, and I was dragged through two swinging doors. They dragged me through the kitchen. I passed an aging longhair smoking pot with a black man in the doorway of the walk-in cooler.

"More random violence," said the longhair, inhaling.

"I used to work in Cicero, Illinois," said the black man, accepting the joint. "You'd see this ever day."

Two dark-haired men in white were arguing.

"Tebble Six wants sushi too," said one, a Pakistani.

"Two sushi?" asked the other, a Mexican illegal.

"No no no," sighed the Pakistani. He shrugged at me as I went by. "He doesn't understand me. I don't understand him. This is the America of tomorrow."

I heard the clang of a big iron door thrown open. Cold winter air cut through my thin Italian suit. I shivered. Olga and Sunder dragged me to my feet and threw me into a snowbank.

"So long," said Sunder.

"Farewell," said Olga.

They raised tiny weapons. I drew my harmless Bic. They hesitated.

"Drink leaden death!" I screamed, and fired. They dove to each side as a wet umbrella of red ink exploded with a plop in the air between them, and I was running down the alley just as fast as my worn soles would carry me.

Bullets plucked at my expensive sleeve. I needed a tailor. I needed a bodyguard. My shoes slid on the ice and I flew through the air.

As I took flight, I saw, in hideous slow-motion, Olga and Sunder running my way, gracefully and smoothly, their weapons raised. They weren't even breathing hard, the jerks. They left my vision as I completed my somersault.

In flight I saw before me, through quick clouds of my frozen breath, a long silver sleigh drawn by wolves. At the reins, a mysterious smile on her lips, was "Susan." She was bathed in white fur, and she shook the reins as I flew through the air, and the sleigh pulled slowly forward.

I landed in the seat next to her, in a pile of soft fur and down. Her cool hand drew a quilt over me, and her obedient wolves began to run, pulling us swiftly across the icy tundra, toward the distant ring of fire on the plain.

top ten motifs of ian shoales' perfect world

1. Stars (real, imagined, reflected, movie)

2. Wolves

3. Bad food and drink

4. Old girlfriends

5. Fools

6. Disguises

7. Beds

8. Moving vehicles

9. Burly workmen

10. Guys named Sarge

the witching hour

On, on we drove! Through the ring of fire! Past the old oil and abandoned wheat fields, past the broken Burma Shave signs, riddled with buckshot, past the shy Northern people, peering at us from the comfort of their heated cars, past the drifters and truckers and busted families, the real-estate brokers and suckers and jokers, the guys in the pickups and the wild wild girls, French inhalers, the dentist's daughters, past all the boys who dream of merging with those bright lights, of entering that city beyond the plain, same as it ever was. We left them behind.

Zigzagging through buttes, the full moon a beacon above us, the full moon dancing on the sheet of snow that stretched to the horizon, I lay, bundled up.

Every once in a while I would glance up at "Susan," but she would not meet my eyes. She cracked her supple whip, and the wolves moved on.

"Where are we going?" I asked.

"You have something we want," she said.

"Who's we?" I asked, though I had an inkling. I nursed my inkling. I inkled in that bitter cold, drawing the quilt around me. We came to a grade and slid into an arroyo. A smooth stream of ice vanished up into its twists. We came to a stop.

A man was kneeling at the arroyo, a fishing line cast down into a hole chopped in the ice. He was dressed for the weather, in a lightweight parka that gleamed silver in the shining moonlight. He shook his head and turned to us. It was Wilkie, former CEO of ProCorGenTel.

"Will there be anything else, sir?" asked "Susan."

"Not right now," said Wilkie. "Wait. Bring me a cup of coffee, will you?"

"Yes sir, Mr. Wilcox," she said. She walked off into the darkness.

"Once a boss always a boss," I said in disgust. "Look, pal, I don't care who you are or what you're in charge of, it is not part of the job description of an executive secretary to bring the executive his damn coffee. What, are you helpless? You can't walk to the coffee machine and get it yourself? No wonder you guys are prime candidates for coronaries. I suppose you have her pick up your dry cleaning too?"

"She's not my secretary," said Wilkie. "I gave all that up."

"Oh, right," I said. "You came to Montana to go fishing. Well, you're a long way from Montana, bud."

"Not that far," he said. "About five miles, actually. Gee, look at that sky."

The horizon was filled with the northern lights, those strange phosphorescent muscles that move like silent lightning across the frozen night.

"You found Ruth?" he asked.

"Yeah," I said.

"I knew she'd bring you," he said confidently. "As soon as my research revealed she'd sat next to you in college, I signed her with Destiny. It was all a part of the plan. What does Ian Shoales enjoy most in life? Women and television."

I had to admit the truth of his statement. "Susan" returned with two coffees. I could have gone for a cup myself, or at least a donut, but I was damned if I was going to beg.

" 'Susan' is, of course, your actual old girlfriend," said Wilkie. "Number Four, I believe, by your count. We met at an Assertiveness Training Seminar. That's where we hatched our plan."

"Oh," I said. "You have a plan?"

"The end of the world," said Wilkie.

"Why all the disguises and chases and narrow escapes?" I said. "Why didn't you just seize your Destiny yourself?"

I knew what his line would be before he even said it.

"You're going to die anyway," he said. "I don't mind telling you."

"So tell me," I said.

"Well," he said, "it's no fun watching a pot unless it's boiling."

I waited for him to say more, but that seemed to be it.

"Come here a second," he said. I walked to his side. He pointed down, into a hole he'd made in the ice.

"When you use your imagination," he said, "and of course the resources available to you when you run both a major corporation and a covert domestic operation sanctioned by a top secret government organization, anything is possible."

"What am I looking at?" I asked.

"An alternative history of America," said "Susan." "We call this one Number Five."

"Good title," I said. "Poetic." I looked down, and this is what I saw:

an alternative history of america

The streambed was dry. Full moon and northern lights filled the cavern between ice and stream bottom to illuminate a tiny landscape. It was the world, spread out flat like a map in a junior high civics class.

"Number Five," Wilkie said in my ear. "There's New England. Great Britain defeated us in the American Revolution, when they wised up and sent some real soldiers into the fight. Everyone who signed the Declaration of Independence was hung for a traitor. Their bodies hung for weeks on poles outside Philadelphia. There's Haiti. Napoleon gave up trying to defend it. The natives gained their own sovereign state. By 1886, the time of the American Rebellion, they were wealthy enough to send money and troops to the black rebels of America. Later, of course, World War I would erupt. Black men would fight black men to shake off the yolk of Haitian tyranny. Like it?"

"I dunno," I said. "What else is on?"

"Number Seven," said Wilkie. The landscape shifted. "We win the revolution. There's the great American slave revolt of 1814, led by the great cruel Zulu leader, Shaka, who'd been captured as a slave. The slaves used *voudou* to great effect. A plague of terror rendered the Southern whites immobile, and the South became a system of tribes. After a hundred years of uneasy truce with the North, a tribal delegation met in St. Cloud, Minnesota, and the generous black people gave the precious gift of rock and roll to their pale white brothers and sisters. Peace reigned thereafter."

"What did they get in return?" I asked.

"Sturdy brooms," said Wilkie. "Chairs. Scientific breakthroughs."

"For rock and roll? Not an even trade," I said. "Even here, the white folks win."

"Try Number Nine," said Wilkie. "The Mormons establish a separate nation in Utah. They defeat Texas in 1860. Mexico in '66. World War I ignites when they try to convince the Prince of Alabama that he is the cursed son of Ham."

"Who won the war?" I asked.

"Nobody ever wins," said Wilkie. "Look there, in that little container, the brave astronauts Lincoln, Armstrong, and Goode circle the moon. They circle the dead rock in the sky forever."

He put his arm around my shoulder.

"I have dozens to choose from," he said. "Now all I have to do is make them real. Where is the Destiny Commander?"

Dozens of lines went through my head ("You're mad I tell you mad," etc.), but I discarded them all, and said, "I lost it."

"You lost it," repeated Wilkie.

"You were always losing things," said "Susan."

"It's an inconvenience," said Wilkie. "Still, I still have the top secret plans. I'll just have to make another."

"May I kill him now?" asked "Susan."

Wow! She *really* knew how to nurse a grudge.

"By all means," said Wilkie. "But do it back around the bend, will you? I need to think."

"Susan" removed a sleek blue-black Kessler .350 from the folds of her fur coat. "If you'll follow me, sir," she said too politely.

"Good-bye, Mr. Shoales," said Wilkie.

"Wait," I said. "I'd like to know. What are you, a CEO, a fed gone wrong, a Soviet agent, a madman bent on world conquest, what?"

"Just a humble fisherman," said Wilkie. "Maybe if I'd taken a vacation once or twice, things would have turned out different."

"*Ian,*" said "Susan." She goosed me with the gun.

"Yeah yeah yeah," I said. I walked ahead of her, my hands in the air, my eyes on the ground, trying to find a way out of this pickle. How did hopeless situations first come to be known as "pickles"? There's nothing the *least bit* picklish, in my opinion, about walking to your doom in a frozen wasteland, with a bitter ex-girlfriend holding a powerful weapon at your back. There is no interface between abject terror and pickles, the whole thing is—I stopped dead in my tracks.

There, at my feet, half buried in the snow, I could make out the vague shape of the Destiny Commander. It must have fallen here when I threw it from the plane!

"Will you hurry *up!*" said "Susan." "You're so slow sometimes. It used to drive me crazy."

"I uh," I said. "I need to tie my shoes."

"Hurry up then," she said.

I bent over Destiny Commander, and turned it on. To my immense relief, a red light came on, and flickered feebly.

"What are you so mad about?" I asked "Susan," still bent over.

"Men," she said. "They never know. They never learn. They leave the toilet seat up. They only bring you flowers if they think you hate them. They have no conception of the nuances of love—"

I could hear the hammer click back. I whirled, aimed the Destiny Commander at her, and changed the channel. I must confess I hoped she'd turn into a dragon, or a werewolf—someone or something a little more exotic—but she remained outwardly the same. She merely dropped her weapon and said, "What a fool I've been! Ian, forgive me," and rushed to my arms.

"Forget it!" I said, sidestepping her gesture. "We did this forgiveness dance almost twenty years ago, and look where it got us. It's a broken record, babe. Throw it away and give me your purse."

"Anything, my Ian," she said.

Now, every woman with a purse has a pocket mirror in it. I rummaged around till I found hers, a cheap plastic job from Woolworth's, but it would have to do. I intended to point Destiny Commander at the mirror, and turn it on. Theoretically, if my hunch was correct, this would set up a field of Video Feedback, neutralizing all fantasies and (I hoped) waking me up.

But I could hear the buzz of snowmobiles coming nearer across the frozen wastes. My pursuers! They were following the wolf tracks to Wilkie's lair. I didn't have much time. I turned on Destiny.

"Hi Des," I said tenderly.

"Watch that first step," said Destiny. "It's a doozie. Daffy Duck. Forty-seven? Batteries low. Good morning Mr. Phelps. I've made some mistakes in the past, Dave. I want to father a child with Julie Christie. Ow. Danger, Will Robinson."

"Try to focus, Des," I said. "Can you review your systems for me?"

"I'm a fiendish thingie," said Destiny Commander.

"Sure you are," I soothed.

"Mr. Shoales!" came the voice of Ted the Fed from the darkness. "Good job, Ian. We'll take it from here. If you'll just step into the light we'll finish you off. I mean, give you a special medal."

A gunshot echoed. A ricochet made a series of whines, like a coyote on the run.

"Ow," came the voice of Burst from the darkness. "There goes my other leg."

"Whom do you wish me to seduce?" shouted Olga from somewhere.

"System Two," said Destiny Commander. "Video One. TV. Channel Selecter—"

"Belay that," I ordered.

I could hear the swift crunch of footsteps in the snow.

"It's mine!" shouted Fiskel Yahr. "And I mean to have it!"

"System—" I pondered. Which system did I want? "Six."

"System Six," said Destiny Commander. "Lights. Kitchen. Bath one—"

"Nah," I said.

Gunshots were coming faster now.

"Hi Wilkie!" said "Susan." "Over here. We're going to watch some television. Hope you brought the popcorn."

"Got ya!" shouted Sunder.

"Missed me!" shouted Ted the Fed.

"Never did!" shouted Sunder. "Cheater!"

"Try Seven," I said. "Hurry."

"System Seven," said Destiny Commander. "Code required."

"Here we go," I muttered, as Wilkie grabbed me by the neck and pulled me backwards.

"You can't stop me!" he hissed. "Nothing can stop me now!"

"Fuzzbuster," said Destiny Commander. "Doors, General. Global Search. Computer Access. All machinery. Bombs—"

"Bombs," I said.

Dmitri leaped from the darkness and grabbed Wilkie's throat.

"You are the master of disguise?" he shouted. "No! *I* am the master of disguise!"

They clutched each other's throats and rolled into the arroyo. The white lines of tracer bullets stitched across over my head, like the pattern of a radioactive spiderweb.

"Enter code," said Destiny Commander. "Quickly, please, or install new batteries."

"G-O-N-E F-I-S-H-I-N," I said. I hoped my hunch was right.

"Code is incorrect," said Destiny.

"Ow," came a fed's voice.

"Ow," said Sunder.

"F-I-S-S-I-O-N?" I asked.

"Colder," said Destiny.

"I'm bleeding!" shouted Fiskel. "Get my doctor on the speakerphone!"

"W-A-K-E-U-P?" I asked, fishing. Paydirt. Destiny glowed, and its image in the mirror glowed back, and a tiny third glow took shape in the space between the reflected and the real, and the glow began to grow.

The explosion of a hand grenade flared and died.

"Whee! Ow!" came the voice of Ted the Fed, and then the warm wind of a growing force took me, and I was sailing, sliding backwards down the ice.

"Bye Ian," said "Susan." The wolves were howling. I struggled to my feet. No easy task, pals and gals. I'd only ice-skated once in my life. I'd fallen on my butt in front of Dolores, the smart girl in the neck brace, who sat in front of me in my fourth-grade class, and I'd never tried it again. Somehow, though, I remained upright. I was gaining speed, faster and faster.

On my left, in the bleak treeless landscape, the glow of this warm fireball revealed a circle of figures filling each other full of bullet holes. They shivered with impact and shook with the cold, a spaghetti Western left out to freeze. In seconds they were behind me.

On my right, television figures appeared: blow-dried lawyers, women in deep trouble, and tired cops who'd seen it all, soap-opera architects, and cartoon animals, all skating backwards across the ice.

"Destiny!" I shouted above the roar of the wind. Ahead of me I could see the slights of Moscow, and above the lights, tearing the roof off the Circus, a mushroom cloud was growing, like a puff of mutant cotton candy growing at the fair.

"Bombs off!" I shouted. "Bombs! Off!"

Something lifted me off my feet. *Ruth*, I thought. *Ruth. Hold on. I'm coming. Hold on. I'm coming.*

future perfect

And it's the midnight hour here at the Perfect World of Wax, time once again for *Bedtime Realities,* sensual paraffin parables intended for the delight and education of adults—say, there aren't any kids in here, are there?

No, Mr. Shoales.

Gimme some houselight, Sarge. You aren't adults. What are you?

We're a Cub Scout troop, Mr. Shoales.

Please let me stay. My parents said it was okay.

I'm almost thirteen, sir!

Awright, kid, awright. Leggo of my leg. Let go! All right. Kill the bedroom, Sarge.

Awwww.

We're going to the Circus.

Aw.

You kids sit down and keep quiet before I change my mind. Bring up the Circus, Sarge!

Ooooooh!

There's the Circus, kids. One push of the Destiny Commander and the whole world leaps into life.

Is that really the whole world, sir?

No it's not really the *whole world.* I can't squeeze the *whole world* into a space the size of eight football fields, no matter what scale I use. You gotta leave *something* out. But I fit in most of it. In the grandstands overlooking the arena, families from around the world! See the tiny flashbulbs pop!

Cool!

There in the balconies, the jet-setters and stars, and foreign dignitaries. Only the heaviest of bribes could get you a spot in the balconies. Ornate, huh? Hand-carved. There's the loge—secretarial pools, stockbrokers, production assistants, and undersecretaries of state—a great place for singles to mingle, so I was told. But you don't know about that yet. I know—too much.

And there, surrounding the arena, in the raked clay pits, the riffraff of the earth, standing room only, the gypsies and drifters, their breath making clouds. Even that packed humanity can't make a dent in the winter cold. They kick up dust impatiently with their feet. They're waiting for the spectacle. They want to feel their hearts pound in their chests.

And there, depicted on the cyclorama in back, is everybody who couldn't get in: the poor, the starving, the tortured, the fierce warriors who will fight to the bitter end—people to whom a Circus means less than nothing. The third world. The vanishing tribes. The dying.

You can examine the murals at your leisure. But now—

Drumbeats and trumpets. The tramp of thousands of marching feet. From the East, the Red Army! From the West, *our* fighting men, dressed in sensible khaki. Here come the huge scarlet tanks, dragging the sleek missiles. Low-flying jets buzz the cheap seats.

Ha ha ha!

You'd duck too, kid.

The armored vehicles wheel in tight circles on the perimeter of the crowd. Red clouds of clay dust churn up under their treads.

Ooooh!

They halt. They take up formations on either side of the big arena. Big fireworks go up—the eagle and the bear ignite the sky!

Wow!

Lower the lens, Sarge. Kids, you'll want to burn the details of this into your memory. Thirty wolves pull the Soviet float into the center of the arena.

How'd you do that?

I didn't, kid. I hired people who did. Each hair on each wolf was tucked into place through a miracle of modern technology. Electron microscopes and lasers, operated by cool men with steady hands, fused each and every hair to that lifelike lupine flesh, in an area so tiny glue was useless, areas so tiny they verged on the subatomic.

Lupine?

Wolf-like. Couldn't you infer the meaning from the context of the sentence?

Huh uh. What are the wolves pulling?

The Soviet secret weapon. The Soviet Destiny Commander. As large as a house (in scale, of course). And there's the Soviet leader, riding Destiny to his fate. The crowd roars. The loudspeakers boom amusing propaganda. It's another Soviet trick! The delighted crowd roars its approval.

And here comes our President and his little fat advisers. They've got a scotch in one hand and a briefcase in the other. Registered voters, selected at random, pull the giant missile into place. It dwarfs the Soviet missiles. It's a missile as big as the two World Trade Centers put together.

It's only a foot long, mister.

This is built to scale, kid. Use your goddam imagination. We don't trust the Russians, so the missile is real. But we don't know that our missiles are useless against the jamming rays of Destiny Commander. Doesn't look good for the U.S. of A.!

Cool! This is just like the gunfight at O.K. Corral!

You like Westerns, kid? There's hope for America after all. Ever see *My Darling Clementine*? Henry Fonda and Victor Mature? Best role he ever had. They remade it in the fifties with Burt Lancaster and Kirk Douglas. Not bad. Then there was that incredibly stupid movie with Stacy Keach as Doc Holliday—

We're launching, Mr. Shoales!

Right. The packed crowd thinks it's just a show. But the missile is launched. The Destiny Commander turns on. Our missile falls to earth. But something's gone wrong. It starts to explode (in slow-motion of course, so everyone can appreciate the effect). Listen to that crowd! They're laughing. They think the explosion is a joke! The big Destiny Commander slides off its float, and wheels in stupid circles, sending its rays wildly into the crowd! The crowd goes nuts!

This is the laughter of the undereducated rich who own oil wells. This is the laughter of the sophisticated at the bad manners of the poor. This is the laughter of lowlife trash who poke sticks at small animals behind bars. This is the laughter around the water cooler at jokes about AIDS. This is the laughter at sick jokes. This is the laughter of terrorists as they place electrodes where they'll have maximum effect. This is the laughter that commands: *Send Choppers!* This is the laughter that commands: *Send Bombs!* It's the laughter at the expense of others. It's the laughter of the cruel world. It's the kind of laughter your mother doesn't like the sound of.

My mom doesn't like the Circus.

Most moms don't. The big mushroom cloud goes up. We're going to go down together. The crowd stops laughing. They start to scream in fear. Hear that roar?

Turn it down!

What's the matter, kid, ya scared? All right, all right, hold my hand. Come on, kids, gather round me. There. The big mushroom pushes the roof off the Big Top. The Big Top rips at the seams, catches fire. Big stretches of canvas tear, and fall into the arena. The cold distant stars are revealed in the sky. The stars don't care what happens here. The cold touch of winter creeps, invisible, down.

But wait! What's that sudden warmth? The crowds and armies drop their weapons and souvenirs; they're pressed at the exits, desperate to escape, when suddenly—they stop. The west wall of the big tent is glowing as pink as sunrise! It's a warm glow from the plains of North Dakota, like the promise of spring. Is it—? Can this be—? The final gasp of tiny fading sturdy Destiny Commander? *My* Destiny Commander? Does the American meet the Russian illusion there, under the Big Top? Yes! The tent wall melts like a sheet of wax in the light of the sun.

Yay!

And when that gentle fireball meets the mushroom, they merge, and implode. Like deflated balloons, in fast-motion, they shrink and fall, and as they fall they disintegrate. They turn to specks of glitter, all silvery and gold, until they fall on the assembled heads of the crowd, a benediction from a dead church.

And the billions assembled there accept that benediction. They relax. Applaud. They cheer. They stretch, and go home. They stream out the doors, back to their comfortable hotel and motel rooms, back to their cars for the long drive home. Look there, the long lines of headlights, the containers full of tired moms and dads, the kids already drifting off in the back seat, lulled by the confined space and the hum of the engine, into security. The nightmare is over. Okay Sarge. Shut it down.

Gee that was neat, Mr. Shoales. It wasn't like our history class at all!

What did you learn in your history class?

You saved the world.

And?

You lost the girl.

What girl?

Ruth.

Remember it forever, kids. I want the world to know. Because it's all true. Unscramble it, decode it.

You're hurting my arm, mister.

It's true. Believe me. It's true.

Ow. Leggo Mr. Shoales, you're hurting me.

What? Sorry, kid. To tell a lie in times like these would only break my heart. There she is in wax!

Gosh! She's beautiful, mister.

Turn her off, Sarge. Follow the exit signs, boys. Find your own way out.

ruthless world

———————————— At that precise moment, as American know-how met Soviet, and as the big hiss of their confrontation faded into silence, I slid and skidded to a halt in front of the entrance to Monroe's Doctrine. I could hear the car doors slam in the vast parking lots. I could hear the cries of happy exhausted children in the aftermath of that terrifying yet comforting spectacle.

Self-conscious as always, I lay gasping before those closed forbidding doors, and wondered: *Are these the final pages from some bizarre novel, or the discarded scenario of an old Bob Hope movie? When those doors open will I find Ruth in the arms of Bing Crosby, leaving me alone with some wisecrack as the screen fades to black?* I shivered, dusted myself off. I pounded on the door three times.

"Who is?" came Vladimir's voice. "No Contras here."

"Perfect world," I shouted. "Perfect world. Come *on.*"

The doors opened wide. I stumbled through. The club was empty—deserted. Not to put too fine a point on it: Everyone had gone.

"Where's Ruth?" I grabbed Vladimir by the throat. "Where is she?"

"Gone," said Vlad, sadly throwing me across the room. "Gone back to L.A."

"Gone?" I asked.

In a wink, like a psychic, I could see the future: Lucille's hit single, "Mushrooms Are for Omelets."

Like a spinning headline in an uncolorized movie, a headline stopped and announced: LUCILLE: FOLK SONGS FOR NEW FOLK.

I closed my eyes and cringed at a montage of implications— FOLK-ROCK REVIVAL boomed the news vendors on the street. And there was the *People* magazine article: OLD FOLKIE PENS HITS FOR A NEW GENERATION, with a picture of Ruth holding a pen and a fluffy cat in some Malibu bedroom.

Ruth could see the future too: she could see the lawyers and the agents and the media drag Lucille away. She could see a fluke hit dangle before her eyes. Ruth had to follow after, like a shark in the wake of a pleasure cruise. She was not young, and youth is a virtue in the ethics of pop. This was her photo opportunity, even if she was just a figure in the background of Lucille's glossy. And even if she was just the background in the bar scene of somebody else's movie, it was better than what she had. She was stuck on a label that didn't want her. She was stuck in a world that did not value her. The Serious Songwriter had become a Sensible Woman. Take the hit and run. Ruth had left me Ruthless, seizing her day while its gold remained untarnished.

And who's that man on the runway, with his pockets full of empty dreams?[3] Did he lose the name tags Mom sewed into the lining? Did he burst from the Cub Scouts, cold, into a wicked wicked world? Who is that haggard aging city boy on the cold black tarmac, standing in the drifting dust of a dying city of dreams, who stands in the chill and the cold as the widebodies roar off, as the amputated hands of giants are flung into the sky? It's me, pal. That's who.

[3]Damn, that's good writing.

Hands will receive her at LAX. Her hands will sign contracts, and she will move into that half-life of the jackals of fame. I, the infamous, had been left behind, imagining the best and worst for her, simultaneously. But hey, isn't that what America's all about?

Suddenly I noticed an old woman and her husband, standing next to me on the runway.

"They call that an outfit," she said to me. "Look at that. I call it underwear."

She was pointing at a gaggle of high school girls deplaning for the sights of Moscow, North Dakota. She was wearing an I SURVIVED MOSCOW sweatshirt. Her husband grunted. She turned to me.

"This used to be ours, you know," she said.

"Yeah?" I said.

"Oh ya," she said. "We like to come here from the old folks' home. We watch the planes take off. From the edge of the runway there over to the Circus. That was our farm. Government bought it."

"High time too," said her mate. "Too shittin' cold for farmin'."

"Now Franz," she said. "We watch the planes now. They fixed it up real nice, dint they?"

"Don't know what they come here for. Wear long johns and call 'em outfits. Make things up and fool folks it's real."

"You got no adventure, Franz," she said. "You got no magic in you."

"Magic, huh?" said Franz. "They had this place in olden times we'd all of us be burned for witches."

"Need a ride, young fella?" she said. "We're headin' back to town."

"What's left of it," said Franz. "Most folks gone to Florida. Who'd wanna come here when you got Florida to get to? I dunno. I'm just glad I don't gotta farm this no more. I thank God for small favors."

I climbed in the back seat of their ancient Perfect Studebaker.

"You lie down there, boy," she said. "It's a ways and you need some sleep."

I lie back and lean my head against the vibrating window. A warm voice speaks calmly from the radio, then music fills the car, some bland sad thing with strings, and the old man hums tunelessly along. I blink at buttes and stars. There are stars in the sky, stars reflected in the window. I close my eyes and imagine more. I imagine a future for myself—a desperate man in a rich man's bed, struggling to wake up. I see a world of wax, a widening crack in the roof of that world, I see the hot glare of the sun peep through, and a paraffin dream dissolve in the light of day, to run like a molten river to the sea. Outside a shuttered window, a time machine grinds slowly to a halt, like a blender that's blown a fuse. Good-bye oh Perfect World. Bye-bye clocks in slivers on the floor. Bye-bye bucks that slip through the fingers. Bye-bye broken dreams forgotten with the coming of dawn. Bye-bye rent. Good night, dial tone, you stop that now. Good night, voices with unreasonable demands. Good-bye, good-bye.

There's a gruff voice in my ear: "Are you all right?"

"Yes," I say. "I'm fine."

Hit the snooze bar. Dream.

wake up

———————————— "I'm fine! I'm fine!" I woke up, coughing, in a haze of smoke. "Save *The Last Supper*!" I shouted weakly. "Incredible three-D replica of da Vinci's masterpiece, in wax!"

"Calm down, ya putz," said a gruff soothing voice. Burly hands carried me from Fiskel Yahr's apartment, and dumped me rudely near the pool.

A paramedic leaned over me to ask, "You got insurance?" I pretended to pass out. They fed me air and strapped me down; they loaded me into their emergency van and we all went screaming away.

Well. It seems my makeshift wake-up system (*Timetables of History* weighing down the scan button of Fiskel's remote-control unit) had not only failed to wake me up, but had shorted out, causing *Timetables* to catch fire. My disgusted neighbors had awakened before I had, and dragged me semiconscious from the encroaching flames! It would probably have been thrilling if I'd been awake to enjoy it.

My roommate at the hospital, as it turned out, was Lucille, who was recovering nicely, despite a tendency to cough up pieces of audiocassettes every two hours. R.J. was there too, to hold her hand and glower fiercely when anyone came near. Neither of them recognized me (I was slightly smoke-damaged), which was just as well.

Michael, of Michael and Tatiana, called to wish me well, and to apologize. Tatiana's trance channeler, it seems, had revealed to her that I'd been her prime minister when she had been Queen of Atlantis. So Michael said I could take all the drugs I wanted, so long as I had relatively clear wits during the Perfect World creative sessions. I told him where he could shove their Perfect World.

Fiskel Yahr called, to fire me (even though he was *insured* for fire damage, the cheap bastard). He said he'd sold the warehouses and the monkey-bear demons (batteries not included) with them. Why sell something you don't own, he reasoned, unless you're assured of a profit? I said I understood. As a matter of fact, while I had him on the phone, I asked him what he thought about the concept of a *universal* remote-control unit. A one-unit-replaces-all type thing. He liked the idea, and said he would put his staff to work on it. Though I couldn't really call the idea mine, he bought my suggested name for five thousand dollars: *Destiny Commander*. He messengered the check over.

So I was relatively flush again. I checked out, to the relief of the hospital staff, and bought a one-way ticket to San Francisco. I was still coughing liquid smoke, but I was otherwise okay. I called some people, paid my most pressing debts (though my apartment and possessions were gone), and checked into a motel with cable. I'd apartment-hunt in the morning. I lay down on the bed and spun the dial.

And so, bathed in the glow of the vast wasteland, I end my little book. Every night, folks, I scan the screen, but the media remain Ruthless. I have dreamed since of dead cities far from the sea, and of mushrooms, erupting to blaze me from my sleep, but I have never seen Ruth since that dark dreamy night when I wrote a book, and saved the world, and the hands of the Perfect World took her away.

perfect coda

A Symposium on Perfection was held in the Back Room at Ian Shoales' Perfect World of Wax.

THE PANEL

SOCRATES: Greek seeker after truth
ROLAND BARTHES: French guy
GEORGE WILL: Major dude
IAN SHOALES: Wise guy
SIGMUND FREUD: Viennese quack
CHARLES DARWIN: Father of evolution
WILLIAM F. BUCKLEY: Moderator
HENRY KISSINGER: Special guest star appearing courtesy of the speakerphone

BUCKLEY

We have taken as the subject for this symposium, *Perfection*. Perhaps, in these arguably imperfect times, Perfection is still not unattainable. We will direct our efforts toward that end, to wit: a working definition of Perfection which will be, if not agreeable to all, at least—

SHOALES

Can we get on with this? I got a date tonight.

SOCRATES

So you are impatient.

SHOALES

Yeah.

SOCRATES

Tell me, sir, on your "date" this evening, will you be impatient?

SHOALES

Probably.

SOCRATES

Do you think patience is a virtue?

SHOALES

No.

SOCRATES

Do you think, then, that impatience is a virtue?

SHOALES

I think you should shut up.

WILL

Here, in that Plato's Cave which we call the American Republic—

SOCRATES/SHOALES

Shut up.

FREUD

Perhaps what you call impatience is merely a personality dysfunction. Once one is aware of the reasons for behavior, one can begin to manipulate people in very subtle ways. Did I say *manipulate*? I mean *psychoanalyze*.

SHOALES

Oh, who the hell cares. This sounds like a potential segment on "20/20." Real hard-hitting.

SPEAKERPHONE

Squark blurk.

BUCKLEY

We're having a little trouble with the speakerphone, Henry. I'll try to set up a conference call.

BARTHES

Could you pass the cream, please? And I believe, yes, one of those jelly-filled donuts?

DARWIN

I don't know why I'm here. I don't know what Perfection means. I'm just a bug collector.

BUCKLEY

If we could try to address the issue—

SHOALES

Why don't you try to address an envelope? Haw haw.

BUCKLEY

Your syntax reveals your lack of breeding.

SHOALES

Your syntax reveals your breed is lacking. Ooooh, that's *good*. Gimme five, Roland.

BARTHES

You are joking. Let us consider cream as the Perfect substance. To the bourgeois it is Perfection itself. It removes the ebony from coffee. It is the Apartheid of additives. It thickens what is thin—a bourgeois health-indicator. It is a sexual presence without the danger of real sexuality—

SHOALES

Your java's getting cold, pal.

DARWIN

I have some notes on the sexual habits of angleworms, if that would be instructive.

BUCKLEY

I believe we have the phone working now. Henry? Henry? Can you hear me? Henry?

SHOALES

What about the sexual habits of angleworms?

SOCRATES

Are you then fascinated by the sexual habits of angleworms?

BUCKLEY

Henry? (BANGING SOUND)

SHOALES

Hey, can we call out on that thing? Let's call my mom. She'd get a real kick out of talking to you guys.

DARWIN

You have a mother?

FREUD

How do you feel about that?

WILL

I hate to put a damper on the discourse, but our old friend the economic indicator always rears his ugly head. Who wants to tackle that?

SPEAKERPHONE

Squark blurt greep.

WILL

Anybody?

SHOALES

Oh, hang up on the guy and let's make some toll-free calls.

SOCRATES

Does your date, then, have a friend?

SHOALES

Sure. What are you doing tonight, Charlie?

DARWIN

I am a married man. I will probably order a pizza and watch television.

SHOALES

I know a place that makes the Perfect pizza.

BARTHES

This is "infotainment" at its finest!

SPEAKERPHONE

Brawk.